IN FOCUS 2

A vocabulary-driven, multi-skills critical thinking course

Charles Browne • Brent Culligan • Joseph Phillips

KINSEIDO

Kinseido Publishing Co., Ltd.
3-21 Kanda Jimbo-cho, Chiyoda-ku,
Tokyo 101-0051, Japan

First published 2024 by Kinseido Publishing Co., Ltd.

Book and cover design SunCross Media LLC

Contents

Plan of the book

Unit	Title	Reading texts	Reading skills	Vocabulary	Listening
1 pp. 1–8	A World of English	1 The Wonder of Language 2 An English-Speaking World	Skimming Scanning Checking details Making inferences Identifying opinions	Collocations Word parts: *equa/equi* Example: *equivalent*	Discussion dictation Listen to readings online
2 pp. 9–16	Disappearing Languages	1 The Rise and Fall of Languages 2 The Killer Language	Skimming Scanning Checking details Cause and effect Making inferences	Collocations Word parts: *prim* Example: *primary*	Discussion dictation Listen to readings online
3 pp. 17–24	Where Are All the Babies?	1 Population Pyramids 2 Fewer and Fewer Babies	Skimming Scanning Checking details Reference words Making inferences	Collocations Word parts: *pre* Example: *previous*	Discussion dictation Listen to readings online
4 pp. 25–32	Our Crowded Earth	1 Population Growth 2 Exploding Population	Skimming Scanning Checking details Making inferences Identifying purpose	Collocations Word parts: *ex* Example: *expansion*	Discussion dictation Listen to readings online
5 pp. 33–40	The Price of Excellence	1 Sports and Competition 2 The Search for Speed	Skimming Scanning Checking details Cause and effect Making inferences	Collocations Word parts: *pend/pent* Example: *suspend*	Discussion dictation Listen to readings online
6 pp. 41–48	Do Great Athletes Deserve Great Salaries?	1 The Economics of Sport 2 Salaries of Top Sportspeople	Skimming Scanning Checking details Pronouns Making inferences	Collocations Word parts: *tract* Example: *attract*	Discussion dictation Listen to readings online

| Research skills | Writing | Critical thinking | |
		Skills	Speaking
Information gathering • Identifying loanwords and their meanings Interpreting and reporting results • Comparing meanings • Discussing differences	Writing a short paragraph Pros and cons of English as a world language	Identifying fact or opinion Categorizing statements: positive, neutral, negative	Discussion • Pros and cons of English as a global language • Reaching a group consensus Quotable Quotes • Discussing students' attitudes to use of English
Information gathering • Rating jobs that need English Interpreting and reporting results • Comparing lists • Predicting the future	Writing a short paragraph Pros and cons of English as the dominant world language	Identifying fact or opinion Categorizing statements: positive, neutral, negative	Presentation • English as the Global Language Tip: Use of gestures in presentations Quotable Quotes • Discussing whether everybody in the USA should speak English
Information gathering • Group survey on family size Interpreting and reporting results • Analyzing data relating to population pyramids • Analyzing and explaining charts	Writing a short paragraph Summarizing pros and cons of population changes	Identifying fact or opinion Categorizing statements: positive, neutral, negative	Presentation • Effects of population changes on countries Tip: Presentation structure Introductions and conclusions Quotable Quotes • Discussing implications of low birthrates
Information gathering • Group survey on future family size Interpreting and reporting results • Comparing results with the national birthrate	Writing short statements Consequences of population growing or decreasing	Identifying fact or opinion Categorizing statements: positive, neutral, negative	Discussion • Matching speakers to statements • Discussing the statements and reporting to the class Quotable Quotes • Discussing the decision to have children
Information gathering • Methods to help athletes perform their best Interpreting and reporting results • Comparing methods • Assessing their impact	Writing a short paragraph Expressing an opinion about competition and sports	Identifying fact or opinion Categorizing statements: positive, neutral, negative	Discussion • Considering statements about competition and cheating • Finding out and reporting the majority view Quotable Quotes • Discussing what motivates successful people
Information gathering • Ranking sportspeople students would pay to see Interpreting and reporting results • Comparing sportspeople and sports	Writing a short paragraph Summarizing arguments about paying athletes high salaries	Identifying fact or opinion Categorizing statements: positive, neutral, negative	Discussion • Ranking factors for paying high salaries • Discussing salaries paid for different jobs Quotable Quotes • Discussing the contradictions between sport and money

Plan of the book

Unit	Title	Reading texts	Reading skills	Vocabulary	Listening
7 pp. 49–56	The Inconvenient Truth of Climate Change	1 What Is Global Warming? 2 Hotter and Hotter	Skimming Scanning Checking details Reference words Identifying opinions	Collocations Word parts: *dict* Example: *predict*	Discussion dictation Listen to readings online
8 pp. 57–64	The Global Warming Myth?	1 The Meaning of Myth 2 The Myth of Global Warming?	Skimming Scanning Checking details Identifying reasons Identifying opinions	Collocations Word parts: *pro* Example: *prospect*	Discussion dictation Listen to readings online
9 pp. 65–72	Changing Ideas of Beauty	1 Beauty 2 What Is Beauty?	Skimming Scanning Checking details Cause and effect Making inferences	Collocations Word parts: *dis* Example: *disagree*	Discussion dictation Listen to readings online
10 pp. 73–80	Is Beauty Skin Deep?	1 Improving on Nature? 2 The Never-Ending Desire for Beauty	Skimming Scanning Checking details Cause and effect Making inferences	Collocations Word parts: *poly* Example: *Polynesia*	Discussion dictation Listen to readings online
11 pp. 81–88	Vegetarianism	1 A Vegetable Diet 2 Vegetarianism: The Healthy and Moral Choice	Skimming Scanning Checking details Identifying reasons Making inferences	Collocations Word parts: *kilo* Example: *kilogram*	Discussion dictation Listen to readings online
12 pp. 89–96	Animals as Food	1 Meat Made Man 2 Animal Slaves	Skimming Scanning Checking details Identifying reasons Making inferences	Collocations Word parts: *ab* Example: *abuse*	Discussion dictation Listen to readings online

Research skills	Writing	Critical thinking	
		Skills	Speaking
Information gathering • Carbon footprints Interpreting and reporting results • Comparing the efficiency of different forms of transportation	Writing a short paragraph Summarizing opinions about global warming	Identifying fact or opinion Categorizing statements on a scale	Discussion • Answering questions on aspects of global warming • Reporting results of discussions Quotable Quotes • Discussing effects of global warming on society
Information gathering • Matching movies to disasters Interpreting and reporting results • Discussing why people watch disaster movies	Writing a short paragraph Describing a graph showing changes in the earth's temperature	Identifying fact or opinion Categorizing statements: positive, neutral, negative	Presentation • What is an ideal climate? Tip: Good posture in presentations Quotable Quotes • Discussing the leadership role of the USA on the issue of global warming
Information gathering • Ranking attractive features in people Interpreting and reporting results • Comparing rankings and drawing conclusions	Writing a short paragraph Summarizing opinions about staying beautiful and the money spent on it	Identifying fact or opinion Categorizing statements that the author might make	Presentation • Using questions about the nature of beauty as the basis for a presentation Tip: Openers and closers in presentations Quotable Quotes • Discussing whether beauty is just physical
Information gathering • Group survey on attitudes to physical features Interpreting and reporting results • Comparing survey results about appearance	Writing a short paragraph The consequences of altering one's appearance	Identifying fact or opinion Categorizing statements: positive, neutral, negative	Discussion • How important is appearance in professional life? Quotable Quotes • Discussing making changes in life that are permanent
Information gathering • Meat consumption by students Interpreting and reporting results • Comparing results • Analyzing meat consumption worldwide	Writing short statements Pros and cons of vegetarianism	Identifying fact or opinion Categorizing statements: positive, neutral, negative	Discussion • Considering statements about vegetarianism • Reporting results of discussions Quotable Quotes • Discussing whether an animal's life is as valuable as a human's
Information gathering • Listing animals and their uses Interpreting and reporting results • Comparing lists • Discussing how the use of animals has changed	Writing a short paragraph Arguments for and against using animals	Identifying fact or opinion Categorizing statements: positive, neutral, negative	Discussion • Answering questions related to the use of animals by humans Quotable Quotes • Discussing arguments against keeping pets

Acknowledgments

Charles Browne would like to thank his wife, Yukari, and their three children, Joshua, Noah, and Hannah.

Joseph Phillips would like to acknowledge the support of his family.

Brent Culligan would like to thank his family in Japan and Canada who provided the motivation to take on this project.

The authors would like to thank Richard Walker for his tireless, patient, and positive support throughout the entire writing process.

The authors would also like to thank the entire Kinseido team for their faith in this exciting new chapter in the life of the *In Focus* series, especially Masato Fukuoka, Takahiro Imakado, Kyuta Sato and Alastair Lamond.

Kinseido and the authors appreciate Christopher Wenger and Brian Romeo of SunCross Media for their valuable design contributions.

To the teacher

Welcome to *In Focus*, a multi-level, corpus-informed course aimed at high school and university students. *In Focus* is designed to build all four skills, while also systematically developing knowledge of core vocabulary and students' critical thinking skills. Each Student Book contains 12 topic-based units, which are divided into six general themes. It provides two units in a row on each theme to help better develop students' critical thinking skills on these issues.

In Focus is supplemented by a range of free online learning components, which provide great flexibility and help to speed language acquisition.

We have created a unique lexical syllabus containing the most important words for second language learners of English. The authors of this series are also the creators of the New General Service List Project (www.newgeneralservicelist.com), a collection of corpus-based word lists, each providing the highest coverage in the world for that specific genre. The syllabus for *In Focus 2* is based on the New General Service List (NGSL), a list of approximately 2,800 words that allows learners to understand approximately 92 percent of the words in most texts of general English. These are nearly all the words learners will ever need (not bad, if you consider there are more than 600,000 words in English!). In each level of *In Focus*, 120 of these words are taught in depth (10 per unit). In *In Focus 1* and *In Focus 2*, these words are taken from the NGSL, while in *In Focus Academic 1*, they are taken from the New Academic Word List (NAWL). Students can use the free online tools and resources developed especially for *In Focus* to learn additional unknown words from our NGSL and NAWL word lists.

All readings and written materials are graded to contain a very high percentage (90–95%) of high-frequency words from the NGSL. This helps develop students' reading fluency and confidence.

Though *In Focus* can be used as a standalone textbook, dedicated online elements enable students to personalize and extend their learning beyond the classroom. Among the online components are interactive flashcards, interactive dictionaries that show the keywords being used in authentic video clips, crossword and word search puzzles, speed reading exercises, supplemental graded readings for each unit, vocabulary worksheets, and audio recordings of all reading texts.

In Focus 2 is designed for students at an intermediate level. Each unit is designed to help your students build both their knowledge as well as their ability to think critically about a wide range of important topics. The topics covered are English as a global language, over- and under-population, salaries and drug use in sports, global warming, ideas of beauty, vegetarianism, and factory farming. Language prompts are provided throughout to help students express themselves.

The *In Focus* Teacher's Manual contains full step-by-step teaching notes, unit-by-unit summaries, language notes, tips, extension activities, options for assessment, and a complete answer key.

We hope you and your students enjoy using *In Focus*.

Charles Browne   Brent Culligan   Joseph Phillips

How a unit works

All units in *In Focus* are eight pages long and follow a similar format. An audio icon reminds students they have the option of listening to the reading texts (available free from the website).

Unit organization

	Objective	Section

Page 1	Warm up
	Schema building
	Real-world connections
		1 Critical cartoons
		   Warm up
		   Media link

Pages 2–3	Vocabulary development
	Reading
	Speaking
		2 Core vocabulary
		   Skimming and scanning
		   Words in context: collocations
		   Word parts
		   Discussion dictation

Pages 4–5	Reading
	Reading skills
	Speaking
		3 Reading skills
		   Pre-reading
		   Reading
		   Checking details; Making inferences;
		   Identifying opinions/purpose/reasons;
		   Cause and effect; Reference words; Pronouns
		   Discuss it

Page 6	Gathering, comparing, and analyzing information
	Speaking
		4 Researching a topic
		   Information gathering
		   Interpreting and reporting results

Pages 7–8	Critical thinking skills
	Writing
	Discussion
		5 Critical thinking
		   Fact or opinion?
		   Categorizing
		   Writing
		   Discussion; Presentation
		   Quotable Quotes

Unit sections

1 Critical cartoons

This is a short speaking activity centered on a cartoon related to the topic of the unit. All cartoons are authentic cartoons, and each was carefully chosen to represent the unit topic. Questions help activate schema and develop critical thinking skills.

2 Core vocabulary

Each unit teaches 10 important words from the New General Service List (NGSL). The section begins with a short reading passage (approximately 250 words) on an aspect of the unit topic that contextualizes the 10 keywords. A series of learning activities focuses on developing knowledge of collocations and analyzing and understanding word parts. This gives students practice using the words introduced in the unit. It also develops vocabulary learning skills and strategies that will be useful when encountering new words not introduced in the unit. A speaking activity rounds off this section.

3 Reading skills

Students work with a longer text (approximately 500 words) that gives a different or expanded point of view on the topic of the unit. This exposure to multiple points of view is a key aspect of developing skills in critical thinking. All 10 keywords appear in the second reading as well, providing additional in-context information about how the words are used. This is followed by a series of carefully structured activities including pre-reading, comprehension, making inferences, and identifying opinions. The section culminates in a short discussion.

4 Researching a topic

Since information from various points of view is crucial to thinking critically about an issue, the pair or group activities in this section encourage gathering further information related to the topic. This is followed by interpretation and presentation of the information collected.

5 Critical thinking

Through pair, group, and open class work, students are encouraged to develop critical thinking skills, such as identifying the difference between statements of fact and opinion, comparing information in tables, and categorizing data. A language model helps students to write a short paragraph and express their opinions on the topic. The final page brings the content of the unit together in a discussion or presentation about the topic. Useful language prompts help students where necessary.

6 Quotable quotes

This final section introduces a quote on the topic of the unit, in most cases by a famous person. Several thought-provoking questions on the quote conclude the unit. This section can be done in class as a short discussion activity or as a writing assignment outside the class.

To the student

Welcome to *In Focus*, a multi-level course for high school and university students. We have designed this series to help you build your vocabulary, work on all four basic skills (reading, writing, speaking, and listening), and help improve your discussion and presentation skills. *In Focus* will also help you think critically, which is a very important general academic skill. In each Student Book you will find 12 topic-based units. In addition to the Student Book, there is a range of free online components, which will help you focus on what you really need, learn more quickly, and become a more independent learner.

For *In Focus*, we have created a unique vocabulary syllabus containing the most important vocabulary words for learners of English. This list has a total of about 2,800 words, which are nearly all the words you will ever need. If you know these words, you will understand 92 percent of the words in most texts of general English (not bad, if you think that English has over 600,000 words!). You will learn 120 of these words in each book, 10 per unit. You can use the website and online tools developed especially for *In Focus* to learn the rest of the 2,800 words efficiently and enjoyably. Online, you will find a range of activities such as vocabulary puzzles, games, flashcards, and audio recordings of the reading texts.

In Focus 2 is designed for students at an intermediate level. Each unit will help you build your knowledge about a wide range of interesting topics as well as help you think critically about these topics. You will study and discuss issues such as English as a global language, over- and under-population, salaries and drug use in sports, global warming, ideas of beauty, vegetarianism, and factory farming. In every unit, we also provide you with useful language and expressions where needed to help express yourself better.

We wish you good luck using *In Focus*. We are sure that the book and the online materials will help you to learn English quickly and in a fun way!

Charles Browne   Brent Culligan   Joseph Phillips

"Get off that table!
Don't you understand
plain English?"

In this unit, you will:
- read an article about language development.
- read an article about the English-speaking world.
- discuss the pros and cons of English as a world language.

1 Critical cartoons

A Warm up

Work with a partner or in a small group. Look at the information on this page and the cartoon. Discuss the questions below.

1 How many countries can you name where English is spoken as a first or second language?

2 Have you ever met an English speaker who expects others to be able to speak English? Why do you think they might have that attitude?

3 Think about the use of English among your grandparent's generation, your parent's generation, and your own. How has it changed?

4 What is the message of the cartoon? What is the connection to the unit topic?

> English is spoken as a first language in ...

> I guess some English speakers think ...

> One way the use of English has changed is ...

> Maybe the message of the cartoon is ...

MEDIA link

Fry's Planet Word (2011) is a five-part documentary series written by actor and writer Stephen Fry. It explores language and its role in human history. Episode 4, "Spreading the Word," examines the influence of English as a world language. It looks at how technology influences language evolution and spread.

For additional media links, go to infocus-eltseries.com

2 Core vocabulary

A Skimming and scanning

1 Find and underline the keywords in the passage. Try to guess their meanings.

Keywords

acquire	equivalent	estimate	exposure	multiple
per	regional	researcher	retain	struggle

The Wonder of Language

We all speak one. Every day, people communicate with one another using language. From the thousands of words we know, we easily find the words we need and arrange them into sentences to 5 give our opinions or make requests. Some researchers who study how we acquire language, like the well-known writer on language Steven Pinker, estimate that people know about 50,000 to 60,000 words by the age of 20. That is roughly equivalent to 10 learning eight or nine words per day from birth.

This amazing process begins from the day we are born. Children who have not yet learned to speak listen to their mothers, fathers, brothers, and sisters talk to them. This early exposure introduces the child to the sounds of their language. This is when they begin to acquire their regional accent. We are all amazed at how little American babies sound American, while 15 little English babies speak with a British accent.

By the time children become three, they have usually learned many thousands of words. Children have heard some words multiple times, so it is not surprising that they know them. Other words children may hear only once, but they retain the meaning. Some words are difficult, and the child has to struggle to say the word but still has no problem remembering 20 its meaning.

Learning a foreign language may be difficult, but it is important to remember that people are born to communicate through speech. It is a gift we all have.

2 Read the statements below. Which best describes what this text is about? Circle A, B, or C. Then explain your answer to a partner.

A How we learn foreign languages

B How children acquire their accents

C How we learn our own language

B Words in context: collocations

1 Look at the text on **page 2**. Find the keywords that form collocations with the words below.

1 researchers _____

2 roughly _____

3 _____ day

4 _____ accent

collocations

Collocations are common word combinations. For example, the verb *express* is often found with the noun *opinion*, as in *express your opinion*.

2 **Match the four keywords with the words below to make new collocations.**

1 _____ costs

2 _____ amount

3 _____ government

4 _____ month

5 average _____

6 cash _____

7 _____ director

8 _____ year

C Word parts: *equa/equi*   Example: *equivalent*

Words with *equa/equi*

adequate   equation   equator   equidistant   equinox   equivalent   inequality

1 Use the words in the box to complete the sentences below. Try to guess the meaning of any words you don't know.

1 A kilogram is roughly _____ to two pounds.

2 When something is _____, it is enough for a situation.

3 A mathematical statement in which both sides are the same is an _____.

4 We can see _____ in a society when groups of people are treated differently.

5 When a place is the same distance from two other places, we can say they are

_____.

6 The invisible line that divides the earth into northern and southern halves is called the

_____.

7 The time when the sun is directly over the equator and night and day are the same length is

called an _____.

2 Work with a partner. What do you think *equa/equi* means? Write your guess below. Then check your answer with another partner.

I think *equa/equi* means _____

D Discussion dictation

1 Listen and write down the questions. Then discuss them in small groups.

1 How _____ ?

2 How _____ ?

3 What _____ ?

2 Form new groups and compare your answers.

A Pre-reading

1 Quickly scan the text and circle the 10 keywords.
2 How many people around the world do you think are learning English?
3 Why do you think English has become an international language?

B Reading

Read the text and check your answers to the pre-reading questions above. Then highlight an interesting idea in each paragraph.

An English-Speaking World

English is widely spoken in many countries around the world and is an official language in more than 50. Many of these countries are former colonies of Britain and retained English after independence. But
5 even Rwanda, the former French-speaking colony of Belgium, has adopted English as an official language.

English has truly become an international language. Researchers at the British Council estimate that it is spoken as a first language by 375 million people
10 and as a second language by another 375 million. Meanwhile, over 750 million people speak it as a foreign language, and this number is growing rapidly. In China, there are an estimated 400 million English language learners. According to the British Council,
15 two billion people around the world are attempting to acquire English, and one in four can speak some English.

When the captain of a Mexican passenger plane flies into an airport in France or Germany, he or
20 she communicates with the air traffic controller in English. It is easy to understand why: the pilot may not speak French or German, the air traffic controller may not speak Spanish, and it is necessary to confirm details about the flight. However, in the equivalent
25 situation, when the same plane lands in Argentina or Colombia, the pilot again communicates with the ground in English, even though both the pilot and the ground controller have Spanish as their mother tongue. This is just one example of how English is
30 used as the standard international language around the world. Today, three-quarters of the world's mail, most books, and many of the world's newspapers and magazines are written in English. More than half of the world's websites are in English, and over 100 new

English websites are created per minute. Eighty percent of international organizations use English as an official language, including the United Nations, the European Union, and the International Olympic Committee. English is the most important language in science: half the world's scientific papers are written in it. Finally, in the world of entertainment, it is impossible to avoid exposure to English. Hollywood movies sell the most tickets in cinemas, and popular songs in countries from Sweden to Japan are sung in English.

English is an international language because of two main regional influences. The first is the rule of the British Empire, which at its peak in 1922 governed a fourth of the world's area and a fifth of its population. The second is the power of American companies that spread around the world after World War II.

English is not just an international language because it is spoken all over the world. English now belongs to the world. People all over the world don't just struggle to learn it to get better jobs. They add words and expressions of their own, and they are changing the language in multiple ways. This helps to make English a true world language. English as a world language allows all countries to be part of the world community, and this benefits us all.

C Checking details

Read the questions below and circle the correct answers according to the text.

1 Which of the following statements is true?

    A There are more speakers of English as a first language than as a second language.

    B The majority of English speakers speak it as a first language.

    C Approximately 25 percent of people in the world can speak some English.

    D Nearly 50 percent of international organizations use English as an official language.

2 Which of the following statements is NOT true?

    A Many former British colonies kept English as an official language after independence.

    B A former French colony has English as an official language.

    C Mexican pilots speak English when communicating with air traffic controllers in Colombia.

    D Most of the world's books are written in English.

D Making inferences

Read the sentences below and circle the correct answers according to the text. (There may be more than one correct answer.)

1 People around the world want to acquire English because ...

    A they want to understand Hollywood movies.

    B air traffic controllers need English.

    C they want better jobs.

    D they want to learn about American companies.

2 Which of these changes are likely to take place in the future?

    A English vocabulary will grow.

    B English won't be spoken at meetings of the Olympic Games Committee.

    C Pilots will choose which language to speak when they are in the air.

    D English will become a world language.

E Identifying opinions

Work with a partner and answer the question below. Check (✓) the boxes.

In this article, how can the author's point of view best be described?

| Paragraphs 1–4 | ☐ positive | ☐ neutral | ☐ negative |
| Paragraphs 5 | ☐ positive | ☐ neutral | ☐ negative |

Discuss it

Work with a partner or in a small group. Ask and answer the questions below.

1 Look back at the ideas you highlighted in the text. Are they the same? What are the differences?

2 Give at least two examples of the spread of English in your country.

3 Are there any languages that could one day compete with English? Explain which language and why or why not.

4 Researching a topic

A Information gathering

1 Work in small groups. Use the pictures below to identify words English has borrowed from other languages. Can you guess which language they came from?

A _____ B _____ C _____ D _____

E _____ F _____ G _____ H _____

2 Think of six words from your language that came from English. Then look up the meaning of the words in English in a dictionary or online. Complete the table below.

Borrowed word	Meaning in your language	Meaning in English
1		
2		
3		
4		
5		
6		

B Interpreting and reporting results

Form new groups and compare your findings. Discuss the questions below.

1 Which meanings are the same in both English and your language? Can you think of any that are different?

2 Why do you think the meaning of some borrowed words is different in your language?

3 Do you think borrowed words help you acquire English more easily? Why or why not?

One word with different meanings is ...

Perhaps the first users of the word didn't ...

We think that borrowed words don't always help because ...

5 Critical thinking

A Fact or opinion?

There are many different points of view on the topic of English. Work with a partner and decide if the following statements are fact (F) or opinion (O).

1 Spanish sounds more beautiful than English.   _____

2 Chinese is the most difficult language to learn.   _____

3 English has more words than most other languages.   _____

4 English has borrowed words from many other languages.   _____

5 British English is easier to understand than American English.   _____

B Categorizing

1 Decide if the following statements sound positive, neutral, or negative. Put checks (✓) in the boxes. Underline any words in the sentences that support your choice.

	Positive	Neutral	Negative
1 English is spoken widely throughout the world.			
2 The spread of English is destroying many languages and cultures.			
3 English as an international language will lead to world peace.			
4 Pilots flying Mexican planes in France or Germany always use English.			
5 It is impossible to escape English in the world of entertainment.			

2 Compare your answers with a partner. Explain the reasons for your choices.

C Writing

Look back at the statements in B above. Write a short paragraph about the positive and negative results of English becoming the world language. Use the model below.

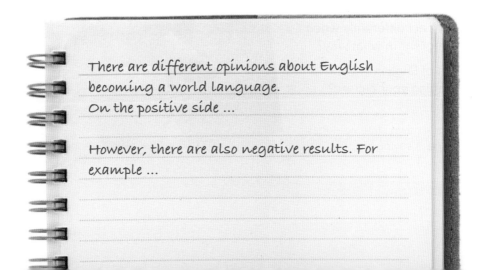

There are different opinions about English becoming a world language.
On the positive side ...

However, there are also negative results. For example ...

D Discussion

1 In C, you wrote about the positive and negative results of English being the world language. Now read the statements below about language from young people around the world. Discuss them in small groups. Do you agree or disagree? Share your opinions and ask follow-up questions.

"English helps speed globalization and economic development. That's a good thing."

"English as a global language gives English speakers an unfair advantage."

"If English spreads everywhere, then so does Western culture. That makes the world a worse place."

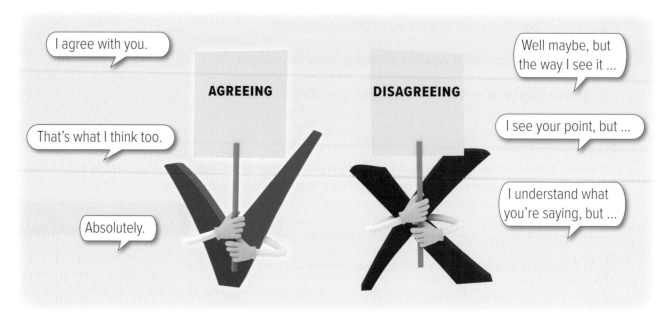

2 Now agree on a group opinion for each point. Share your results with the class. Each group should present one idea.

❝ Quotable quotes
Final thoughts . . . ❞

Learn a new language and get a new soul.

Czech proverb*

1 How is this quote connected to the topic of the unit?

2 Do you feel or act differently when you speak English? In what way?

3 Is the growth of English in your country changing your culture? If so, how?

*proverb (n): a well-known statement that often gives advice; a saying

Disappearing Languages

In this unit, you will:

- read an article about the popularity of different languages.
- read an article about "killer" languages.
- make a presentation on English as the Global Language.

1 Critical cartoons

A Warm up

Work with a partner or in a small group. Look at the information on this page and the cartoon. Discuss the questions below.

1 Does your first language have many English words in it? Give some examples.

2 Does it matter if languages disappear? Why or why not?

3 Why do you think English has become such an important language?

4 What is the message of the cartoon? What is the connection to the unit topic?

> Some English words we use in my language are ...

> I think it matters if a language disappears, because ...

> One thing that makes English important is ...

> I think the cartoon is trying to get us to think about ...

MEDIA link

Language Matters with Bob Holman (2015) is a documentary that asks: What do we lose when a language dies? What does it take to save a language?

For additional media links, go to infocus-eltseries.com

A Skimming and scanning

1 Find and underline the keywords in the passage. Try to guess their meanings.

Keywords

absolutely	administration	cite	collapse	dominate
elementary	outcome	primary	severe	vital

The Rise and Fall of Languages

Many people think about the number of languages in the world today and worry. They see that some languages dominate while other languages are disappearing. In many countries today, students start studying English in elementary school. Some people worry that these students will use their native language less and less. They worry that there will be a severe reduction in the number of people speaking their language and that the language will   5

disappear. Some call on the government to create laws to protect their language. For example, in Canada, the Quebec government administration has passed laws to ban people from using English words on signs. Such people   10 believe that it is vital for the government to work to maintain the primary position of their language and prevent language death.

Unfortunately, there may not be anything people can do to avoid this outcome. Analysts   15 have looked for causes of the decline in the number of languages. They found a mathematical model that explains how things become extinct. The model looks at the rate

of growth between two similar things. It shows that small differences in rates of growth will   20 result in big differences over time. One will collapse while the other will continue to grow. Scientists cite examples such as the extinction of family names and certain kinds of DNA. This model also applies to languages. We can't predict which languages will disappear, but we are absolutely sure that not all languages will be spoken in the future.

2 Read the statements below. Which best summarizes the text? Circle A, B, or C. Then explain your answer to a partner.

   A There are many ways to save a dying language.

   B Mathematics can explain why things become extinct.

   C The disappearance of languages is natural.

B Words in context: collocations

1 Look at the text on **page 10**. Find the keywords that form collocations with the words below.

1 government _____

3 avoid this _____

2 _____ position

4 _____ sure

2 Match the four keywords with the words below to make new collocations.

1 local _____

5 _____ perfect

2 _____ cause

6 whatever the _____

3 favorable _____

7 _____ source

4 _____ right

8 current _____

3 Work with a partner. Use the collocations above to make your own sentences.

1 _____

2 _____

3 _____

4 _____

C Word parts: *prim*   Example: *primary*

Words with *prim*

prima donna   primary   primates   prime   primers   primeval   primitive

1 Use the words in the box to complete the sentences below. Try to guess the meaning of any words you don't know.

1 Elementary school students use simple textbooks called _____ to learn to read.

2 Chimpanzees, orangutans, and humans are all _____.

3 You can eat _____ beef at that restaurant.

4 _____ humans used stone tools.

5 In opera, the main female singer is called the _____.

6 On the west coast of Canada, some _____ forests remain.

7 In England, elementary school is known as _____ school.

2 Work with a partner. What do you think *prim* means? Write your guess below. Then check your answer with another partner.

I think *prim* means _____.

D Discussion dictation

1 Listen and write down the questions. Then discuss them in small groups.

1 What are _____ ?

2 Other than _____ ?

3 Does _____ ?

2 Form new groups and compare your answers.

A Pre-reading

1 Quickly scan the text and circle the 10 keywords.

2 What are the five most widely spoken languages in the world?

3 What do you think the term "killer language" means?

B Reading

Read the text and check your answers to the pre-reading questions above. Then highlight an interesting idea in each paragraph.

The Killer Language

The world's languages are like endangered animals. As the human population increases, farmland and cities expand. Crops grow where there was once forest; animals that live there are then driven into the
5　small wild areas that remain. Animal numbers collapse, and some animals may eventually disappear. A similar process threatens many of the world's languages.

Nobody is absolutely certain, but researchers cite estimates that there are around 7,000 languages
10　spoken in the world today. The most popular are familiar: Mandarin Chinese, English, Spanish, Arabic, and Hindi are the native languages of hundreds of millions of people and are studied by many more. But most of the 7,000 we have never heard of. They are
15　spoken by only thousands of people. Not only are there few speakers of these minority languages, but if we examine who the speakers are, we also find that they are mostly old people.

These languages are
20　disappearing at a rapid rate. In fact, we are seeing the greatest language loss ever. Because most of these languages
25　have no written form, there are no books. As a consequence, students aren't taught them at school and don't have
30　even an elementary knowledge of them. As old people die, the language dies with them. Researchers are trying to record these languages before they disappear. However, most of

Hmong woman—one of an ethnic group from China, Vietnam, Laos, and Thailand, with its own language

them exist in remote places, and, unfortunately, many of them are disappearing without anyone knowing. Some experts predict that half of the languages spoken today will be gone by the end of the century.

Why should this be? Why should a language that has existed for tens of thousands of years suddenly disappear? The answer lies in the fact that in our global world, a few primary languages have come to dominate. We can call these languages "killer languages." English is one of them.

The spread of English around the world proceeded in stages. First came British colonies. English became the official language of administration. For local people, knowing English became a vital asset. English ability gave them status and higher income. As a consequence, many parents chose an English education for their children. These children grew up knowing two languages. In the next generation, knowledge of the original language became poor or lost completely. In today's world, many people are moving from rural areas to cities in order to escape severe poverty. In the process, they often adopt a dominant language, which is often English.

The pace of language loss is increasing, but language loss itself is nothing new. There are many examples in history. Few people speak the Celtic languages that once dominated Western Europe. They remain mainly in Scotland, Wales, Ireland, and northern France. A language can experience a recovery: Welsh is an example. But this is very rare and occurs only in special cases. Unfortunately, it seems that the world's endangered languages will share the same outcome as its endangered animals.

C Checking details

Read the questions below and circle the correct answers according to the text.

1 Which of the following statements is true?
   A Most of the world's languages are spoken by few people.
   B Language loss started with the spread of English.
   C Most languages have both spoken and written forms.
   D Welsh is an example of a language that has disappeared.

2 Which of the following statements is NOT true?
   A English spread around the world in different stages.
   B People who travel around the world often adopt English as their main language.
   C Like English, Celtic languages are known as killer languages.
   D Endangered languages often suffer the same outcome as endangered animals.

D Cause and effect

Understanding why something happens (the cause) and what happens as a result (the effect) is an important reading skill. Work with a partner. Each statement of cause below summarizes part of the text. Find the relevant part of the text and in each case describe the effect that results.

Cause	Line	Effect
1 Farmers cut down trees to plant fields.	_____	_____
2 Most of the world's languages have no written form.	_____	_____
3 Elderly speakers of endangered languages die.	_____	_____
4 A few main languages dominate.	_____	_____
5 English ability leads to higher pay and more respect.	_____	_____
6 People move from the country to urban areas.	_____	_____

E Making inferences

Read the sentences below and circle the correct answers according to the text. (There may be more than one correct answer.)

1 Non-English-speaking parents might choose to educate their children in English because …
   A they like living in the city.
   B they don't want English to disappear.
   C they want their children to get better jobs.
   D half of the world's languages will disappear.

2 Urbanization causes languages to die out because …
   A there are few chances to speak minority languages.
   B major languages are mainly spoken in cities.
   C minority languages are rarely used in the business and working world.
   D of all the above reasons.

Work with a partner or in a small group. Ask and answer the questions below.

1 Look back at the ideas you highlighted. Are they the same? What are the differences?

2 Would you move to an English-speaking country for a better job or lifestyle?

3 What are your reasons for learning English?

4 Researching a topic

A Information gathering

Work in small groups. Make a list of 10 very different types of jobs. Then rate each one on a scale of 1 to 10, depending on how important English is to the job (1 = not important at all; 10 = essential).

How important is English?	
Job	**Rating (1-10)**

B Interpreting and reporting results

Form new groups and compare your lists. Discuss the questions below.

1 How many jobs need some English? How has this changed over the past 50 years?

2 Where will English be needed more in the future? Why?

3 What industries don't need English? Why?

> One thing that has changed is ...

> It's difficult to predict, but ...

> One area where English will be needed more is ... because ...

> I think it's obvious that ...

> I'm not too sure if/whether ...

> One thing is certain ...

5 Critical thinking

A Fact or opinion?

1 There are many different points of view on the topic of English and other languages. Work with a partner and decide if the following statements are fact (F) or opinion (O).

    1 Humans created farms and cities out of forests.   _____

    2 Hundreds of millions of people speak Arabic, English, and Spanish.   _____

    3 Half of all languages will disappear by the end of the century.   _____

    4 English is a language for people with high status and income.   _____

    5 The speed at which we are losing languages is increasing.   _____

2 Now write two more statements about this topic—one fact and one opinion. Then show them to another pair and ask them to say which is fact and which is opinion.

    1 _____

    2 _____

B Categorizing

1 Decide if the following statements sound positive, neutral, or negative. Put checks (✓) in the boxes. Underline any words in the sentences that support your choice.

	Positive	Neutral	Negative
1 The effect of English on other languages is similar to the process of animal extinction.			
2 It's easier to communicate these days because so many people speak English.			
3 Languages that have been around for thousands of years are disappearing quickly.			
4 The expansion of the British Empire helped English become a world language.			
5 Welsh is one of the few languages that has survived the spread of English.			

2 Compare your answers with a partner. Explain the reasons for your choices.

C Writing

There are many different opinions about language dominance and the spread of English. Look back over this unit and write a short paragraph that expresses your opinion. Use the model below.

Today, it is clear that English …

There are both advantages and disadvantages to this. For example …

Overall, I believe that …

D Presentation

Work in small groups. In C, you wrote about the dominance of English around the world. Now use this and the information in this unit to prepare a presentation with this title:

English as the Global Language

Use the structure below and be sure to give examples. Decide who will prepare and present each section.

Introduction
- situation in the world today

Body
- reasons why English is so dominant

- advantages and disadvantages of this situation

- future developments

Conclusion
- brief summary

- group's view about the situation

TIP

Gestures
Gestures can help make your presentation easier to understand and also more interesting for the audience. They provide physical support for the words. A common type of gesture focuses on a number or sequence of events. For example:

There are THREE reasons why we think the spread of English around the world has more negative than positive effects.

Transitions

So far, we've focused on …
Now, I'd like to …

So, the next question is …

Now, I'm going to talk about …

This brings me to my next point.

Quotable quotes
Final thoughts . . .

Our common language is English. And our common task is to ensure that our non-English-speaking children learn this common language.

Bill Bennett
Former US Secretary of Education

1 How is this quote connected to the topic of this unit?

2 Do you agree that all foreigners in the USA should learn English? Should there be laws about this? (Note: the USA has no official language.)

3 In the USA, approximately 13% of people are Spanish speakers. Do you think all Americans should be able to speak Spanish?

Where Are All the Babies?

drastically
(adv): very
much, often
very quickly

It's all due to the birthrate falling drastically...

In this unit, you will:

- read an article about population pyramids.
- read an article about the effects of low birthrates.
- make a presentation on an effect of aging populations.

1 Critical cartoons

> In our culture, babies are sometimes connected with ...

A Warm up

Work with a partner or in a small group. Look at the information on this page and the cartoon. Discuss the questions below.

> I think in ... the birthrate is ...

> My country seems to be similar to ...

1 The bird in the cartoon is called a stork. In many cultures, storks are connected with babies. Is there something similar in your culture?

> I think this cartoon might be about ...

2 What do you know about birthrates in different countries? Check birthrates for South Korea or Italy and compare them with birthrates in Nigeria or Kenya.

3 How does the birthrate in your county compare with other countries?

4 What is the message of the cartoon? What is the connection to the unit topic?

MEDIA link

Misconception (2014) is a film by Jessica Yu. It looks at issues related to global population, including overpopulation in some areas and declining birthrates in others.

For additional media links, go to infocus-eltseries.com

A Skimming and scanning

1 Find and underline the keywords in the text. Try to guess their meanings.

Keywords

era	estate	forecast	household	increasingly
largely	previous	rural	ultimately	wage

Population Pyramids

One way of looking at population change is with a type of graph called a population pyramid. It is called a pyramid because that used to be the most common shape. We can see this shape with Japan's population
5 in 1950 in Chart A. The population was largely young then, and it was the end of an era when most people lived in the countryside. In these rural areas, children often worked together with their parents and helped to produce the food, goods, and household products
10 that the family needed. There were many diseases without cures, and these often killed children, so families were large to increase the chance that some children would live to become adults.

In Chart B, the pyramid for the year 2000 shows a
15 big difference from the previous chart. There are two reasons for this change. First, children increasingly went to school instead of working. Rather than add to the family estate, children became an expense. Second, new medicines cured children's diseases like
20 smallpox, measles, and polio, so large families were no longer needed.

While it is always difficult to give an accurate forecast, it seems that Japan and other countries with similar population structures, such as South Korea,
25 will ultimately have a pyramid like the one in Chart C. The big question is how society will pay for the large number of elderly people. Taxes on workers' wages won't be enough, so we may see major changes in those societies.

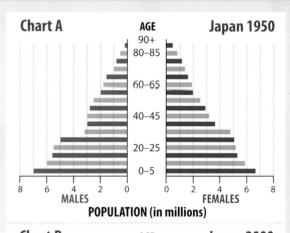

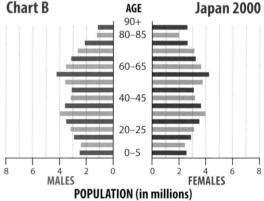

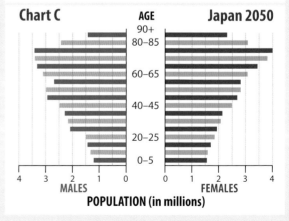

2 Read the titles below. Which would also be a good title for the text? Circle A, B, or C. Then explain your answer to a partner.

  A Childhood Diseases

  B Child Workers

  C Changing Societies

B Words in context: collocations

1 Look at the text on **page 18**. Find the keywords that form collocations with the words below.

  1 end of an _____

  2 _____ areas

  3 accurate _____

  4 workers' _____

2 Match the four keywords with the words below to make new collocations.

  1 weather _____

  2 _____ population

  3 average _____

  4 modern _____

  5 minimum _____

  6 golden _____

  7 _____ development

  8 profit _____

C Word parts: *pre* Example: *previous*

Words with *pre*

precook	predict	prehistoric	prepay	prevent	preview	previous

1 Use the words in the box to complete the sentences below. Change the word form as necessary. Try to guess the meaning of any words you don't know.

  1 I'm really interested in _____ animals like dinosaurs.

  2 A lot of fast food is _____.

  3 Wearing a seatbelt helps to _____ injury.

  4 The weather forecast _____ rain today.

  5 The _____ owner painted the wall red.

  6 A telephone card allows you to _____ for telephone calls.

  7 That movie isn't at the cinema yet, but I saw a _____ on YouTube.

2 Work with a partner. What do you think *pre* means? Write your guess below. Then check your answer with another partner.

I think *pre* means _____.

D Discussion dictation

1 Listen and write down the questions. Then discuss them in small groups.

  1 What _____ ?

  2 Do _____ ?

  3 Do _____ ?

2 Form new groups and compare your answers.

A Pre-reading

1 Quickly scan the text and circle the 10 keywords.
2 Which parts of the world have growing populations? Which countries have fewer children per mother?
3 What problems could countries with fewer children have?

B Reading

Read the text and check your answers to the pre-reading questions above. Then highlight an interesting idea in each paragraph.

Fewer and Fewer Babies

A generation ago, scientists worried about overpopulation. Today, in developed countries, there is the opposite fear. The Total Fertility Rate (TFR) is a measure of the number of children a woman

5 has during her life. The replacement rate is the TFR required to maintain the population. In developed countries, this number is 2.1, but in most of these countries, rates are less than this. South Korea, for example, has a TFR of 0.8. Italy and Japan are at

10 1.3. Internationally, more than 50 percent of people live in countries where the TFR is lower than the replacement level.

There are several reasons why couples are having fewer children. Chief among these is the cost of

15 education. Jobs in developed countries increasingly require highly educated workers, and the cost of this education is largely borne by parents. Another reason is the growth of cities. As people move from rural areas to cities, there is pressure to limit family size.

20 The high cost of real estate means that living space is limited, and there is no room for a large family. In previous eras, a single-wage earner was able to support a household. Today, it is usually necessary for both parents to work. Without childcare that parents

25 can afford or the help of grandparents, couples may not want to have many children. Another reason for the low birthrate is increased equality between men and women. This has resulted in economic independence for many women. As women gain

30 independence, many choose to follow careers and have children later. The wide availability of the birth control pill and access to abortion in many countries

means they can more easily choose when or if they want to become a parent.

There are two results of a TFR that is too low to maintain 3 a population. The first is that, ultimately, without the arrival of immigrants, the population will decline. In over 20 countries, the population is already in decline, including Russia, Ukraine, and Japan. In other countries, such as South Korea, it soon will be. Given present trends, Ethiopia 4 will have a larger population than Japan by 2050. The second and more troubling result is population aging. Fewer and fewer young taxpayers will be supporting more and more old people. This will place even more pressure on young people to limit family size. If there are too few 4 workers, this will cause economic decline.

In the United States, differences in fertility rates won't just lead to a falling population. The TFR of non-Hispanic white Americans is 1.6, while that of Hispanics is 1.9. Along with immigration, this means that white Americans are forecast 5 to become a minority by 2044, and Hispanics will make up 29 percent of the population by 2050.

C Checking details

Read the questions below and circle the correct answers according to the text.

1 Which of the following statements is true?

    A Couples are having fewer children because of education costs.

    B Couples are having more children because both parents are working.

    C Couples are having more children because people are moving to rural areas.

    D Couples are having fewer children because grandparents don't want to take care of children.

2 Which of the following statements is NOT true?

    A Italy and Japan both have low TFRs.

    B The population isn't yet in decline in South Korea.

    C The TFR among white Americans is lower than Hispanic Americans.

    D Couples in the US have fewer children than couples in Japan.

D Reference words

The words below are taken from the text. What do they refer to? Write the correct words or phrases on the lines.

1 *this number*   (line 7)   _____

2 *these countries* (lines 7–8) _____

3 *these*   (line 14)   _____

4 *This*   (line 28)   _____

E Making inferences

Read the sentences below and circle the correct answers according to the text. (There may be more than one correct answer.)

1 People in cities have fewer children because …

    A there is a lack of public transportation.

    B there is more crime in the cities than in rural areas.

    C houses are smaller in the city.

    D it's hard to find work in the city.

2 What changes to American society might take place in the future?

    A More people will speak Spanish.

    B There will be many immigrants from Spain.

    C White Americans will disappear.

    D There will be more Hispanics than white Americans eventually.

Discuss it

Work with a partner or in a small group. Ask and answer the questions below.

1 Look back at the ideas you highlighted. Are they the same? What are the differences?

2 The text gives several reasons why couples are having fewer children. Think of your family and friends. Which reasons are true for them?

4 Researching a topic

A Information gathering

1 Form small groups and interview each other. Ask about the number of brothers and sisters your partner and your partner's parents have. Write in the table below.

Name	Brothers	Sisters	Mother		Father	
			Brothers	Sisters	Brothers	Sisters
Total						
Average						
Average per generation						

2 Work out the averages for each column and for each generation.

3 Collect the results on the board in the front of the class.

B Interpreting and reporting results

Form new groups. Discuss the questions below.

1 Look back at the charts on page 18. Which population pyramid best fits your class?

2 Look at the figures below. What are the reasons for the differences among countries?

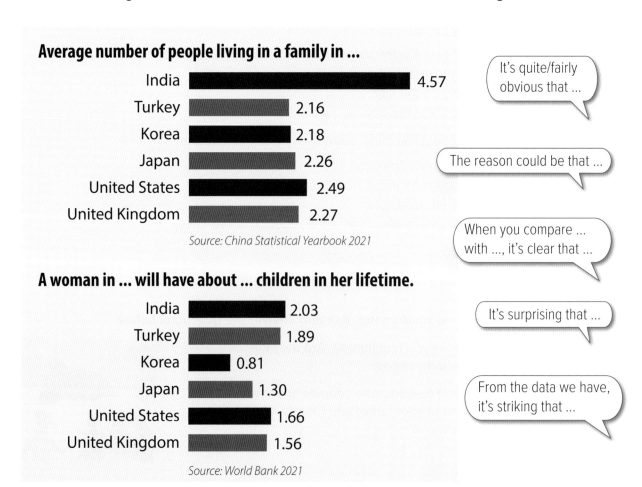

Average number of people living in a family in ...

India 4.57
Turkey 2.16
Korea 2.18
Japan 2.26
United States 2.49
United Kingdom 2.27

Source: China Statistical Yearbook 2021

A woman in ... will have about ... children in her lifetime.

India 2.03
Turkey 1.89
Korea 0.81
Japan 1.30
United States 1.66
United Kingdom 1.56

Source: World Bank 2021

It's quite/fairly obvious that ...

The reason could be that ...

When you compare ... with ..., it's clear that ...

It's surprising that ...

From the data we have, it's striking that ...

5 Critical thinking

A Fact or opinion?

There are many different points of view on the topic of birthrates and population. Work with a partner and decide if the following statements are fact (F) or opinion (O).

1 Raising children is too expensive. _____

2 If the birthrate is 2.0, the population will decline without immigration. _____

3 Older people don't pay enough tax. _____

4 In 2020, white Americans were a majority of the population. _____

5 The birthrate in the United States is too low. _____

B Categorizing

1 Decide if the following statements sound positive, neutral, or negative. Put checks (✓) in the boxes. Underline any words in the sentences that support your choice.

	Positive	Neutral	Negative
1 An open immigration policy helps countries solve many of the problems caused by a low birthrate.			
2 The unreasonably high cost of real estate means that living space is very limited.			
3 As women gain equality and independence, they are free to pursue careers and postpone childbirth.			
4 Economic decline will occur when there are too few workers to support the economic activity.			
5 The US government forecasts that white Americans will be a minority by 2044.			

2 Compare your answers with a partner. Explain the reasons for your choices.

C Writing

Look back at the statements in A and B above. Write a short paragraph about the positive and negative results of population changes in your country. Use the model below.

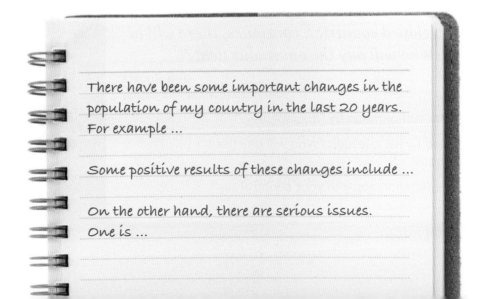

There have been some important changes in the population of my country in the last 20 years. For example ...

Some positive results of these changes include ...

On the other hand, there are serious issues. One is ...

D Presentation

1 Work in small groups. Discuss the paragraphs you wrote in C. Share your opinions and ask follow-up questions.

2 With present trends, developed countries will have small populations and undeveloped countries will have large populations. What will be some effects of this? Think about the topics below. Choose one and prepare a short presentation in your group.

- Education
- Immigration
- Employment
- Pensions and retirement
- Healthcare
- Poverty
- Housing
- Young people

3 Present your ideas to the class. Prepare your introduction and conclusion carefully.

TIP

Structure your talk

A good presentation will always include three parts. Use these parts and create a general plan before you think about the details:

- **Introduction:** this is where you welcome the audience and state your purpose.
- **Middle section:** this is the main body of the talk.
- **Conclusion:** this is where you summarize the key points and bring everything together.

Introductions

Today, I'll be talking about ...

We'll first look at ...
Then ... And finally ...

The purpose/aim of this presentation is to tell you about ...

Conclusions

So, to summarize the main points again ...

The key issues we have looked at are ...

Let's review the key points. First ...

Quotable quotes
Final thoughts ...

If the current birthrate, which is one of the lowest in the major developed countries, continues, there will be no Japanese. Who will pay the enormous debt?

Jim Rogers
American investor and author

1 What does the author mean by "no Japanese"?

2 What is implied by his question "Who will pay the enormous debt"?

3 Does Japan's situation apply to your country?

In this unit, you will:
- read an article about overpopulation.
- read an article about population growth.
- identify and discuss statements about declining birthrates.

1 Critical cartoons

A Warm up

Work with a partner or in a small group. Look at the information on this page and the cartoon. Discuss the questions below.

1 Which countries have the largest populations? Where does your country rank?

2 What is happening to your country's population? What are the main reasons for this?

3 What do you know about the problems of overpopulation?

4 What is the message of the cartoon? What is the connection to the unit topic?

I think ... has the largest population.

In my country, the population is ...

Overpopulation can cause ...

I think the cartoon is making the point that ...

 **MEDIA link**

Planet of the Humans (2019) is a documentary produced by Michael Moore. It looks at overpopulation and the environmental footprint of renewable energy.

For additional media links, go to infocus-eltseries.com

A Skimming and Scanning

1 Find and underline the keywords in the passage. Try to guess their meanings.

Keywords

critic	decade	expansion	guarantee	launch
overall	reduction	secure	settlement	southern

Population Growth

Overpopulation happens when there are too many people for the food and resources available. This can occur when there is an expansion of the population. It can also happen when there is a reduction in the food produced on farms.

There have been many examples of local overpopulation. However, the idea of world
5 overpopulation was first described by Thomas Malthus in 1798. He looked at population growth in European settlements in North America. He predicted that those settlements would outgrow their food supply in the future. Malthus believed that populations were controlled in two ways. The first way was by increasing the death rate through war or death by hunger. The second way was by lowering the birthrate. His critics disagreed. They pointed out that populations could
10 grow if they could guarantee their food supplies.

In the over 20 decades since Malthus's book, the argument still continues. The world has seen massive increases in its population in countries like China and India. However, many people argue that the overall situation is good. Our
15 food supply has become more secure in two ways. First, by using science, companies launched the era of industrial farming. They have greatly increased crop yields. Second, we transport food from all over the world. For example, we take food from countries in the southern half of the world
20 to the large populations in the northern half, where it is needed. It seems that Malthus is no more correct now than he was in 1798.

2 Look at the pictures below. Which picture goes best with the text above? Circle A, B, or C. Then explain your answer to a partner.

A

B

C

B Words in context: collocations

1 Look at the text on **page 26**. Find the keywords that form collocations with the words below.

1 population _____

2 _____ disagreed

3 _____ food supplies

4 _____ situation

5 _____ the era

2 Match the five keywords with the words below to make new collocations.

1 _____ an attack

2 _____ fast delivery

3 _____ impression

4 rapid _____

5 _____ argue

3 Work with a partner. Use the collocations above to make your own sentences.

1 _____

2 _____

3 _____

4 _____

5 _____

C Word parts: *ex*   Example: *expansion*

Words with *ex*

| exclude | exile | exit | expand | expel | export | expose |

1 Use the words in the box to complete the sentences below. Change the word form as necessary. Try to guess the meaning of any words you don't know.

1 Scientists believe the universe is _____.

2 Brazil _____ many of its products to countries all over the world.

3 In case of fire, use the emergency _____.

4 Tom was _____ from school for cheating on the test.

5 Napoleon was _____ to the island of Saint Helena.

6 As the tide went out, the beach was _____.

7 Many items are taxed, but school supplies are _____.

2 Work with a partner. What do you think *ex* means? Write your guess below. Then check your answer with another partner.

I think *ex* means _____.

D Discussion dictation

1 Listen and write down the questions. Then discuss them in small groups.

1 What may _____ ?

2 What could _____ ?

3 Does _____ ?

2 Form new groups and compare your answers.

A Pre-reading

1 Quickly scan the text and circle the 10 keywords.

2 The world's population has increased by 400 percent over the last 100 years. Why do you think this has happened?

3 Why do some countries have high birthrates and others not?

B Reading

Read the text and check your answers to the pre-reading questions above. Then highlight an interesting idea in each paragraph.

Exploding Population

The world population reached one billion in 1804, after many thousands of years of slow increase. Over the next two centuries, it increased by a factor of seven, reaching seven billion in 2011. And after just 11 more years, it stood
5 at eight billion. Along with people, there has also been a huge expansion in the numbers of domestic animals: there are now more cattle, pigs, sheep, and chickens than at any previous time.

This rapid increase in the number of people was made
10 possible first by farming itself, and then, much more recently, by scientific advances in farming. According to one researcher*, the world population probably never went over 15 million before the development of farming. Farming made possible settlements and reliable food
15 supplies. Staying in one place with the guarantee of food meant more babies survived. This led to a population increase. Much later, in the middle of the last century, the "green revolution" applied scientific methods to farming and greatly increased yields. The result is the population
20 increase we have seen over the last six decades.

Some scientists suggest that it is time to launch a second green revolution. They want to do this by changing the genes of crops. However, critics argue correctly that we are reaching the limits of being able
25 to feed the world and that population growth must stop. They say that the effect on resources is not only due to increased population. As poorer countries develop, people want to eat more meat. More and more land is used to grow crops for animal feed. And overfishing
30 means that some seas are now empty of food fish.

It is true that there has been a reduction in the rate of population growth over the last 50 years. Several European countries, South Korea, and Japan now have very low birthrates that point to population decline.

However, although the pace of the world's population **3** increase has gone down, the total population has increased. Birthrates in some countries, particularly poorer countries in the southern half of the world, remain high for several reasons. First, poor countries often do not have support systems to take care of the **4** elderly. Having many children helps provide a secure old age. Second, many children die before becoming adults.

Population growth is high in many developing countries, but these countries have a lower effect on **4** resources overall. In 2000, an American consumed over six times more resources than a person living in China. However, by 2021, the number fell to two as Americans consumed 32% less and Chinese consumed more. **5**

In the time it has taken you to read this article, around 700 babies have been born. We are clearly coming to the limit that our world can support. It is time to face reality and tackle this problem.

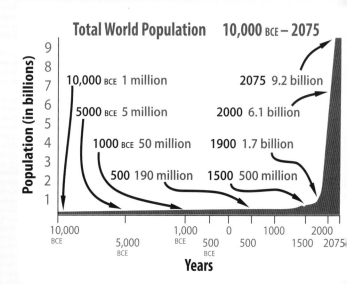

Total World Population   10,000 BCE – 2075

10,000 BCE 1 million
5000 BCE 5 million
1000 BCE 50 million
500 190 million

2075 9.2 billion
2000 6.1 billion
1900 1.7 billion
1500 500 million

Population (in billions)

Years

*Luc-Normand Tellier (2009)

C Checking details

Read the questions below and circle the correct answers according to the text.

1 Which of the following statements is true?

    A Populations in all wealthy countries have fallen.

    B Scientific methods have allowed farmers to grow more crops.

    C Developed countries with lower birthrates have a low effect on resources.

    D Chinese people are now bigger consumers than Americans.

2 Which of the following statements is NOT true?

    A Along with humans, the population of cattle and pigs has also increased.

    B Without farming, the world population would be smaller.

    C The green revolution was a twentieth-century political movement.

    D The population in Japan is shrinking.

D Making inferences

Read the sentences below and circle the correct answers according to the text. (There may be more than one correct answer.)

1 Before the development of agriculture, people got food by ...

    A moving from place to place.

    B raising domestic animals.

    C developing permanent settlements.

    D staying in one place.

2 China consumes more resources than Americans because ...

    A many Chinese people are rich.

    B Chinese have larger families.

    C China has many natural resources.

    D China has over four times as many people.

E Identifying purpose

1 Look at the statements below. Which best describes the author's main purpose in writing the text? Check (✓) the correct box.

☐ To summarize the history of the world human population

☐ To explain how agriculture has affected the world population

☐ To encourage us to do something to reduce the world's population

2 Compare your answers with a partner.

Work with a partner or in a small group. Ask and answer the questions below.

1 Look back at the ideas you highlighted. Are they the same? What are the differences?

2 The second-to-last paragraph talks about how much Americans consume. Is the situation similar in your country? Give specific examples. Some ideas to think about: home, transportation, food, shopping.

4 Researching a topic

A Information gathering

1 Form groups of five or six. Interview each other. Ask how many children, if any, you would each like to have in the future. Write the information in the table below.

Name	Number of children wanted
	Total:
	Group average:
	Class average:

2 Working as a class, add your totals and find out the average number of children your group and the class would like to have.

B Interpreting and reporting results

Discuss the questions below with a partner.

1 What is the replacement birthrate for a country? (See the text in Unit 2 on page 20.)

2 Is your class average above or below the replacement birthrate? How might this affect the future of your country?

3 Why do some people want a big family? Why do other people want only one child or no children?

Expressing possibilities

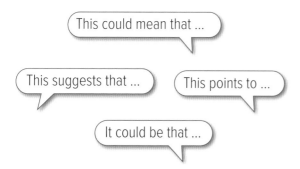

This could mean that ...

This suggests that ...   This points to ...

It could be that ...

Describing and explaining figures

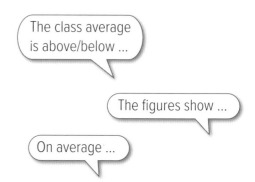

The class average is above/below ...

The figures show ...

On average ...

5 Critical thinking

A Fact or opinion?

There are many different points of view on the topic of birthrates and population. Work with a partner and decide if the following statements are fact (F) or opinion (O).

1 Large families are happy families. _____

2 People in developed countries use more resources. _____

3 Many people in developing countries believe large families provide security in old age. _____

4 A world population of eight billion is too large. _____

5 The current population growth can't be maintained. _____

B Categorizing

1 Decide if the following statements sound positive, neutral, or negative. Put checks (✓) in the boxes. Underline any words in the sentences that support your choice.

	Positive	Neutral	Negative
1 Overcrowding leads to disease.			
2 Science will solve the problems of overpopulation.			
3 Education is lacking in some developing countries.			
4 The planet can support up to 15 billion people.			
5 There will be a population collapse in the near future.			

2 Compare your answers with a partner. Explain the reasons for your choices.

C Writing

Look back at the statements in A and B above. Think about the consequences of the two alternatives below. Write statements for each alternative. Use the model below.

Limiting or reducing the world population:
If we can ..., there will be ...

Allowing the world population to continue to grow:
If we don't ..., one result will be ...

D Discussion

1 In C, you wrote about the consequences of global population changes. Now read the statements from the two people described below. Who said what? Check (✓) the boxes.

Person A: a government minister in charge of improving the country's weak economy.

Person B: a company employee with no children who lives in a crowded city.

Statement	Person A	Person B
1 "Having children is too expensive. I want enough money to enjoy my life."		
2 "If we let the population decrease, there won't be enough tax to pay for all the services people expect."		
3 "We need a larger population to support all the old people."		
4 "Being a parent is just so much work. I'm tired already."		
5 "Unless we add more people to the workforce, we can't compete with other countries."		
6 "There are already too many people for the world to support."		
7 "Everything is so crowded. There is no space. We need fewer people not more."		
8 "New laws should encourage young people to marry and have children."		

2 Work in small groups and compare your answers. Explain your choices.

3 Which statements do you agree or disagree with? Why?

4 Report your results to the class. Overall, which do you think is better: limiting the population or allowing it to grow?

> Person A argues that ...

> I'm not sure if/whether ...

> I don't agree. It seems to me ...

> Person B complains about ...

> Person A points out that ...

> That's exactly what I think.

Quotable quotes
Final thoughts . . .

If motherhood doesn't interest you, don't do it. It didn't interest me, so I didn't do it.

Katharine Hepburn
American actor

1 Do you agree with the statement?

2 Do you think having a family—or not having a family—is just a matter of personal choice? Or are there other things to consider? If so, what are they?

The Price of Excellence

In this unit, you will:

- read an article about sports and competition.
- read an article about drugs and performance in sport.
- discuss how competition affects our lives.

1 Critical cartoons

A Warm up

Work with a partner or in a small group. Look at the information on this page and the cartoon. Discuss the questions below.

1 What sports competitions have you watched or taken part in?

2 Do you think it is important to win at sport? Why?

3 What sports have problems with athletes cheating?

4 What is the message of the cartoon? What is the connection to the unit topic?

> A few months ago, I took part in a ...

> In my opinion, winning is ...

> I think cheating is quite common in ...

> I think the point of this cartoon is to ...

MEDIA link

Icarus (2017) is an Oscar-winning documentary about doping in sport. It focuses on state-sponsored doping in Russia.

For additional media links, go to infocus-eltseries.com

A Skimming and scanning

1 Find and underline the keywords in the passage. Try to guess their meanings.

Keywords

| ban/banned | boost | consequence | current | extremely |
| facility | historic | suspend | tournament | yield |

Sports and Competition

From the fields of war to the fields of sport, humans have always had a strong desire to win. Over 2,500 years ago, Greeks would suspend fighting to come together and compete against each other in the ancient Olympic Games. These tournaments from long ago had many of the sports we have in our current games, like running and jumping. The stadiums that modern athletes compete in are similar to the facilities used by those athletes. Our marathon comes from what people believe to be a historic event, in which a Greek runner ran with an important message from the plains of Marathon to Athens, a distance of about 42 kilometers. According to the story, the runner died as a consequence of his great effort. 5 10

The competitive spirit continues to this day. Many modern athletes are willing to do just about anything in order to win and increase their medal yield. Some are willing to take drugs that boost their ability—even when these drugs are extremely dangerous. One famous case was the Canadian runner Ben Johnson, who ran 100 meters in 9.79 seconds in the 1988 Seoul Olympics. It was later found that he had taken a banned drug, which led to Johnson being banned from Olympic sports. 15 20

2 Read the titles below. Which would also be a good title for the text? Circle A, B, or C. Then explain your answer to a partner.

A Winning at Any Cost

B The Marathon

C Ancient and Modern Sports

B Words in context: collocations

1 Look at the text on **page 34**. Find the keywords that form collocations with the words below.

1 _____ fighting   **3** _____ dangerous

2 _____ event   **4** _____ drug

2 Match the four keywords with the words below to make new collocations.

1 immediately _____   **5** temporarily _____

2 _____ buildings   **6** _____ funny

3 _____ on smoking   **7** _____ political parties

4 _____ victory   **8** _____ cold

3 Work with a partner. Use the collocations above to make your own sentences.

1 _____

2 _____

3 _____

4 _____

C Word parts: *pend/pent* Example: *suspend*

Words with *pend/pent*

appendix	depend	pendant	pending	pendulum	penthouse	suspend

1 Use the words in the box to complete the sentences below. Change the word form as necessary. Try to guess the meaning of any words you don't know.

1 You can _____ on Sunhee. She's a very reliable worker.

2 That old clock has a long _____.

3 The light is _____ from the ceiling.

4 The doctor removed the patient's _____.

5 Vivian is wearing a beautiful _____.

6 Mr. Williams lives in a _____ with views of the river.

7 Paulo's application to join the golf club is _____.

2 Work with a partner. What do you think *pend/pent* means? Write your guess below. Then check your answer with another partner.

I think *pend/pent* means _____

D Discussion dictation

1 Listen and write down the questions. Then discuss them in small groups.

1 What _____ ?

2 What _____ ?

3 What _____ ?

2 Form new groups and compare your answers.

A Pre-reading

1 Quickly scan the text and circle the 10 keywords.

2 Athletes are running faster today than they did a generation ago. What are the reasons for this?

3 Is the world record for the 100-meter race below or above 10 seconds?

B Reading

Read the text and check your answers to the pre-reading questions above. Then highlight an interesting idea in each paragraph.

The Search for Speed

Speed is exciting, especially in sports. In running, the fastest race is the 100-meter dash. It appears that we haven't yet reached our limit when it comes to running. Each time we have set an imaginary barrier, it has been
5 broken. It is likely that we will be surprised and excited when new records are broken in the future.

In a historic moment at the 1936 Olympic tournament in Berlin, Jesse Owens won an Olympic gold medal in the 100-meter dash, with a time of 10.6 seconds. It was
10 thought that a time of 10 seconds would never be beaten. The current record stands at 9.58 seconds, set by Usain Bolt of Jamaica. In a similar historic way, Roger Bannister broke the four-minute barrier for the mile in 1954.

However, the question remains, just how fast can humans
15 run? The answer lies in a combination of several factors. First, there is the physical structure of the runner's muscles. Depending on their structure, some muscles react either quickly and with great power, or they don't supply so much power but they can continue to work over a long period. As a consequence, sprinters
20 tend to have more of the former, while distance runners have more of the latter. In addition to the structure of the muscles, an athlete's body shape also affects performance. Successful distance runners tend to be extremely thin but have large hearts and lungs.
25 Sprinters, on the other hand, are heavily built and over the years have tended to get larger. Training yields improvements in a runner's performance, and so does diet. Professional athletes practice weight and speed training, eat foods high in protein and carbohydrates,
30 and they avoid fats.

In the search for speed, some athletes may use performance-enhancing drugs, which can build muscle or increase the number of oxygen-carrying red blood cells. These methods may be effective
35 in boosting an athlete's performance, but they are banned in competition. An athlete caught using them can be suspended from future tournaments, sometimes for life. However, in spite of the serious penalties, some athletes still use these drugs. There
40 are two main reasons for this. First, in some sports, it may be difficult to compete at the top level without using drugs to boost performance. Second, new drugs that are difficult to detect are always becoming available, and facilities to detect them may not yet exist.
45 There is a cat-and-mouse game going on between athletes and sports authorities. As authorities ban one drug, another takes its place. The result of this is that honest athletes are at a disadvantage. Sports authorities should realize that it is impossible to
50 control this behavior. I believe they should give up their attempt to control drug taking and allow athletes to use any substance they want. In this way, all athletes would have the same chance to compete at the top level.
55

C Checking details

Read the questions below and circle the correct answers according to the text. (There may be more than one correct answer.)

1 Which of the following statements is true?

    A Jesse Owens's Olympic record has never been beaten.

    B Roger Bannister was not a sprinter.

    C People have two basic kinds of muscle for running.

    D Sprinters are sometimes heavily built.

2 Which of the following statements is NOT true?

    A Sports authorities are sometimes banned from competition.

    B Sprinters today are larger than sprinters in the past.

    C Professional athletes don't eat a lot of fat.

    D Some runners use drugs in order to run faster.

D Cause and effect

Read the statements below and decide which are causes and which are effects. Write C (cause) or E (effect).

1 Long-distance runners need a strong supply of oxygen.   _____

2 Some athletes take banned performance-enhancing drugs.   _____

3 New drugs that are difficult to detect are appearing on the market.   _____

4 Athletes are under a lot of pressure to win.   _____

5 Sports authorities test athletes for banned drugs.   _____

6 Long-distance runners often have large hearts and lungs.   _____

E Making inferences

Read the sentences below and circle the correct answers according to the text. (There may be more than one correct answer.)

1 Which of the following is true?

    A Roger Bannister won an Olympic gold medal in 1954.

    B Eating spaghetti and meatballs helps increase athletes' performance.

    C A sprinter needs a large heart and lungs.

    D Roger Bannister ran faster than Jesse Owens.

2 Some athletes take performance-enhancing drugs because …

    A bigger muscles allow you to run faster.

    B without them, they think that they wouldn't be able to win.

    C they can't control their own behavior.

    D they want these drugs to be available to the general public.

Discuss it

Work with a partner or in a small group. Ask and answer the questions below.

1 Look back at the ideas you highlighted. Are they the same? What are the differences?

2 Do you agree that performance-enhancing drugs should be legalized? Why or why not?

3 In what other areas of life do people take drugs to improve performance or reduce stress? What do you feel about this? Think about university life, work situations, leisure, and traveling.

4 Researching a topic

A Information gathering

Many rich countries have budgets and programs to help their athletes perform their best on the world stage. These athletes have advantages that athletes in poorer countries don't have.

1 Work in small groups. Look at the methods shown below. How effective do you think they are? Write 1 to 5 below (1 = most effective; 5 = least effective). Add your own ideas.

Performance-enhancing method	How effective? (1–5)	Class average
Drugs		
High-tech clothing		
High-tech shoes		
Special diets		
Sports drinks		
Training at altitude		
Training facilities		
Vitamins		
Your idea:		
Your idea:		

2 Work with your classmates. Compare your tables and work out the class average for each method. Complete the column.

B Interpreting and reporting results

Discuss the questions below with your classmates.

1 Which method is ranked most effective? Which is least effective? Why?

> ... was most effective. This is probably because ...

> Similarly, ... can be effective.

> In my view, ... is the least effective.

> It was difficult to choose between ... and ... because ...

2 Do you think that professional sports are more exciting because athletes have some of these advantages? Why or why not? Are any of these advantages unfair?

> Despite the fact that ...

> Without doubt, athletes ...

> Most of us felt that ...

> Even though ...

> The majority of us think ...

5 Critical thinking

A Fact or opinion?

1 There are many different points of view on the value of sports in society. Work with a partner and decide if the following statements are fact (F) or opinion (O).

1 The marathon is more exciting than the long jump. _____

2 The Olympic Games are a waste of money. _____

3 Training can improve athletic performance. _____

4 Performance-enhancing drugs should be banned. _____

5 Usain Bolt is a record-breaking Jamaican runner. _____

2 Now write two more statements about this topic—one fact and one opinion. Then show them to another pair and ask them to say which is fact and which is opinion.

1 _____

2 _____

B Categorizing

1 Decide if the following statements sound positive, neutral, or negative. Put checks (✓) in the boxes. Underline any words in the sentences that support your choice.

	Positive	Neutral	Negative
1 High school runners are faster today than Olympians of 50 years ago only because they cheat by using drugs and supplements.			
2 Professional runners avoid eating fat.			
3 World records in running today are much fairer than in the past, since races are not allowed on very windy days.			
4 Some athletes wear special clothes in order to run faster.			
5 Athletes can be suspended if they use drugs. These athletes harm the reputation of their sport.			

2 Compare your answers with a partner. Explain the reasons for your choices.

C Writing

Look back over this unit and write a short paragraph that expresses your opinion on the value of sports and competition in society. Use the model below.

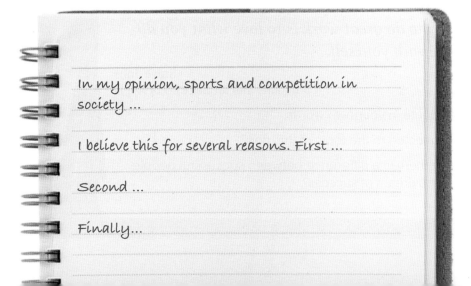

In my opinion, sports and competition in society ...

I believe this for several reasons. First ...

Second ...

Finally...

D Discussion

1 In C, you wrote about the value of sports and competition in society. Now read the statements below about competition and cheating from Simon, Anne, and Miki. Who do you think said what? Check (✓) their names.

Simon Lee
a rich, successful businessman
who owns a soccer club

Anne Green
a teacher who believes that
teamwork builds character

Miki Mori
a recreational athlete who likes
to exercise to stay in shape

Statement	Simon	Anne	Miki
1 "Drugs should be allowed in sport. It's who wins that's important."			
2 "Cheating is acceptable as long as it doesn't harm other people."			
3 "There must always be losers in any competition. That's life."			
4 "Exams just cause stress. They don't bring out the best in students."			
5 "Serious sport is not about fair play. It's about jealousy, violence, and breaking the rules—war, in other words."			
6 "Competition makes people work hard. Without it, there would be no progress."			

2 Work in small groups. Compare your answers and explain your choices. Which statements do you agree or disagree with? Why?

3 Report the results of your discussion to your classmates. How many people in the class think that drugs in sport should be legalized? How many believe that competition in society has more positive than negative effects?

Asking for clarification

What does ... mean exactly?

I'm sorry, I'm not sure I understand the question.

Could you please repeat your question / what you said?

Could you explain that to me once more?

I didn't get your last point.

66 Quotable quotes
Final thoughts . . . 99

The only way to do great work is to love what you do and compete with yourself.

Steve Jobs
Co-founder and former CEO of Apple

1 Explain the quote in your own words.

2 How is it connected to the topic of this unit?

3 Do you think there is a difference between successful people and those who dream of success?

Do Great Athletes Deserve Great Salaries?

"We're offering twenty million plus incentives over a four-year period, Mrs. Morton. Can Timmy come out and play?"

incentive (n): something that encourages a person to do something

In this unit, you will:

- read an article about the economics of sport.
- read an article about the salaries of top athletes.
- discuss salaries for different occupations and whether they are fair.

1 Critical cartoons

A Warm up

Work with a partner or in a small group. Look at the information on this page and the cartoon. Discuss the questions below.

1 Which sports in your country are popular? Has this changed in recent years?

2 Who are the most famous athletes in your country? Do you know how much they make?

3 Why do you think the salaries of professional athletes are so high?

4 What makes the cartoon funny? What is the connection to the unit topic?

> In my country, ... is very popular.

> One of the most famous athletes is ...

> I think one reason the salaries are so high is because ...

> This cartoon is funny because ...

MEDIA link *The Last Dance* (2020) is a 10-part documentary series that chronicles the rise of the Chicago Bulls in the 1990s, with a particular focus on Michael Jordan's final season with the team in 1997–98.

For additional media links, go to infocus-eltseries.com

A Skimming and scanning

1 Find and underline the keywords in the passage. Try to guess their meanings.

Keywords				
analysis	annual	budget	compensation	controversial
debt	profit	recruit	revenue	sum

The Economics of Sport

Unlike amateur athletes, who don't get paid for playing, professional athletes expect financial compensation. At the lower levels, this compensation may not be so much. At higher levels, athletes usually get paid annual salaries whether they perform or not. The amounts can be so high that some people get angry about them. These controversial salaries are the result of market forces that many people don't fully understand. One way to explain it is to study the numbers from professional sports clubs.   5

These clubs earn money in many different ways. They sell tickets and souvenirs to fans. They sell the games to television companies. And they sell products like caps, shirts, and even   10
computer games. The sum of all this gives the total revenue of the club. Then there are the expenses. The club spends money on salaries and facilities. They spend money to recruit new players for the team. The plan for revenues   15
and expenses is the budget, and any revenue left over after the expenses is the profit. But if expenses are greater than revenues, the club will go into debt.

The writers of the book *Soccernomics* used a type of investigation of these figures called a   20
statistical analysis. They compared different figures in the budget with the actual revenues. They found that players' salaries best predicted revenues. In other words, players with high salaries attracted more fans, and the clubs sold more tickets and television time. In short, fans want to see famous players.

2 Read the titles below. Which would also be a good title for the text? Circle A, B, or C. Then explain your answer to a partner.

  A Making Sense of Sports Salaries
  B Rich Athletes
  C Playing for Money

B Words in context: collocations

1 Look at the text on **page 42**. Find the keywords that form collocations with the words below.

    1 financial _____   **4** go into _____

    2 _____ salary   **5** statistical _____

    3 total _____

2 Match the five keywords with the words below to make new collocations.

    1 generate _____   _____   **6** chemical _____

    2 deep in _____   **7** tax _____

    3 _____ vacation   **8** workers' _____

    4 pay off a _____   **9** data _____

    5 full _____   **10** _____ cost

3 Work with a partner. Use the collocations above to make your own sentences.

    1 _____

    2 _____

    3 _____

    4 _____

    5 _____

C Word parts: *tract* Example: *attract*

Words with *tract*

abstract	attract	contract	distract	extract	traction	tractor

1 Use the words in the box to complete the sentences below. Change the word form as necessary. Try to guess the meaning of any words you don't know.

    1 Seil had to sign a _____ when he bought a cell phone.

    2 She had to shout to _____ the waiter's attention.

    3 The dentist _____ Sara's tooth.

    4 Picasso is famous for his _____ paintings.

    5 Valerie was _____ by a phone call and didn't notice the boy crossing the street.

    6 Luis plans to buy a new _____ for the farm.

    7 My car can't climb this hill in the winter; the tires can't get _____ on the ice.

2 Work with a partner. What do you think *tract* means? Write your guess below. Then check your answer with another partner.

    I think *tract* means _____.

D Discussion dictation

1 Listen and write down the questions. Then discuss them in small groups.

    1 What is _____ ?

    2 What do you think _____ ?

    3 Have you ever _____ ?

2 Form new groups and compare your answers.

3 Reading skills

A Pre-reading

1 Quickly scan the text and circle the 10 keywords.

2 Why do some athletes get paid so much money? Think of at least two reasons.

3 How long is the average career of a professional athlete?

B Reading

Read the text and check your answers to the pre-reading questions above. Then highlight an interesting idea in each paragraph.

 # Salaries of Top Sportspeople

When many people are in debt and struggling to meet budgets, it is hardly surprising that Americans complain about the high salaries of some professional athletes. The average annual income in the United
5 States is around $55,000 a year. Some of the highest-paid sportspeople earn more than 2,000 times this amount.

Generally, top-level soccer and basketball players
10 receive the highest salaries. A case in point is the soccer player Lionel Messi, who received compensation of $130
15 million in 2022. Close behind was the basketball player, LeBron James, who made $121.2 million. Of the top ten earners in 2022,
20 seven were soccer or basketball players.

Can these huge sums be justified? Is what these athletes do worth 1,000 times more than the work of
25 a nurse, a doctor, or a teacher? Many people would say that it is not. But it is hard to judge the worth of what someone does; it depends on one's values. An economic analysis of an athlete's pay may lead us to a more balanced and less controversial answer.

30 Athletes sign contracts with team owners, who operate the team as a business. This business is like any other. Let's compare it with a car dealership, and let's also assume that the main purpose for both businesses is to increase profits. The car dealer

who wants to make a bigger profit might expand the business by hiring more sales staff. The team owner can't add more players to the field. A baseball team has nine players—no more, no less. So, the only way that an owner can increase revenue is by attracting more fans, more sponsors, and more TV network contracts. The obvious way to do this is by winning. To win and continue to defeat competitors, the team must recruit the top players, and, unlike car salespeople, these are very rare.

As with any attractive item—gold, diamonds, Picasso paintings—rarity means a high price. Athletes would also point out another difference: the typical career of a top athlete is around 5 to 10 years. This is very short compared with that of a car salesperson.

It is surprising that often those who complain about athletes' salaries are the same people who make those huge salaries possible. They do so by purchasing season tickets and attending games. They do so by watching the games. They do so by buying items with the team's name, such as hats and bags. And they do so by reading about the sport in magazines and newspapers. Choosing not to do these things would be a sure way to stop the "shocking" salaries.

C Checking details

Read the questions below and circle the correct answers according to the text.

1 Which of the following statements is true?

   A In 2022, the highest-paid sportsperson was a basketball player.

   B Seven of the top-ten earners in 2022 were soccer players.

   C A top athlete can expect to earn an income for 10–15 years.

   D Watching games supports high athlete salaries.

2 Which of the following statements is NOT true?

   A Some athletes earn more than 2,000 times the average annual income.

   B The top basketball player made more money than the top soccer player in 2022.

   C Lionel Messi earned around $130 million in 2022.

   D One way for car dealers to increase profits is to hire more salespeople.

D Pronouns

What do the pronouns in bold refer to? Write on the lines below.

1 *Many people would say that **it** is not.*   (lines 25–26)   _____

2 *... **it** depends on one's values.*   (line 27)   _____

3 *Let's compare **it** with a car dealership ...*   (line 32)   _____

4 *... **these** are very rare.*   (line 43)   _____

E Making inferences

Read the sentences below and circle the correct answers according to the text. (There may be more than one correct answer.)

1 Some sportspeople get paid a lot of money because ...

   A ticket prices are becoming more expensive.

   B baseball teams have a fixed number of players.

   C there are very few top players in their sport.

   D they win many games or competitions.

2 Team owners ...

   A run their teams as a business.

   B can increase profits only if their team wins.

   C hire more players to attract more fans.

   D can make more profits by cutting player salaries.

Discuss it

Work with a partner or in a small group. Ask and answer the questions below.

1 Look back at the ideas you highlighted. Are they the same? What are the differences?

2 Compare top sportspeople with other high earners, such as bankers and film stars. What is similar or different?

3 Are any other things as important as profit for the team owner? If so, what?

4 Researching a topic

A Information gathering

1 Make a list of six famous sportspeople and the sports they play.

2 Rank each sportsperson by how much you would like to see them in person (1 = most; 6 = least).

3 Imagine that you have $1,000 to spend to see any or all of these sportspeople. How much would you spend on each person?

Sportsperson	Sport	Rank (1-6)	How much I would pay

B Interpreting and reporting results

1 Work in small groups. Discuss the questions below.

   1 Compare your lists of sportspeople and sports. What are the similarities and differences?

   2 How much would you pay? Compare your amounts.

2 Discuss the questions below with the class.

   1 Which sportspeople are ranked the highest? What is the average amount you would pay to see them?

   2 Do you think your results are related to the salaries paid to these sportspeople? Why or why not?

5 Critical thinking

A Fact or opinion?

1 There are many different points of view on the topic of money and sport. Work with a partner and decide if the following statements are fact (F) or opinion (O).

1 Professional athletes' salaries are much too high. _____

2 Sport fans buy tickets and go to games. _____

3 The highest compensation should go to the best players. _____

4 Messi won the FIFA Ballon d'Or soccer award. _____

5 Messi is the best player in the world because he won the FIFA Ballon d'Or. _____

2 Now write two more statements about money and sport—one fact and one opinion. Then show them to another pair and ask them to say which is fact and which is opinion.

1 _____

2 _____

B Categorizing

1 Decide if the following statements sound positive, neutral, or negative. Put checks (✓) in the boxes. Underline any words in the sentences that support your choice.

	Positive	Neutral	Negative
1 Most professional athletes are highly paid.			
2 Society spends too much money on professional sports, including athletes' salaries.			
3 Players' salaries are set by market forces.			
4 Athletes performing at the highest level are amazing.			
5 It is awful that sportspeople make more money than doctors.			

2 Compare your answers with a partner. Explain the reasons for your choices.

C Writing

Write a short paragraph that summarizes the arguments about paying high salaries to athletes presented in this unit. Use the model below.

Many people object to …

It is clearly true that …

We need to consider the fact that …

However, if we look at sport as business …

D Discussion

1 Work in small groups. In C, you summarized the arguments for and against paying top sportspeople very high salaries. Now read the list of factors below that affect how high a salary is.

   1 Take turns explaining each factor to your partners.

   2 Choose three factors that you think are the most important. Tell your partners why you think these are important.

Factors affecting salaries
Creativity
Cost of living
Danger
Working for a famous company
Helping the environment/people
Impact on society

Factors affecting salaries
Popularity
Qualifications needed
Rarity
Size of the market
Skill needed
Value of work

2 Work as a class. Look at the list below. It shows the average salaries of 10 jobs in the United States. Discuss the following questions with your classmates.

   1 What surprises you about this information?

   2 How does this compare with your country?

   3 If you could, would you change any of the salaries? Which? Why?

Job	Average salary (US$)
Restaurant server	26,000
Office clerk	36,000
Construction laborer	42,000
Firefighter	56,000
High school teacher	64,000
Police officer	70,000
Nurse	83,000
Lawyer	128,000
Surgeon	358,000
NBA Player	5,620,000

Sources: US Bureau of Labor; NBA; Medscape Physician Compensation; 2022 data

> One thing that surprises me is the fact that ...

> In my country ... is/are (much) higher/lower than in ...

> If I could, I would change ... because ...

66 Quotable quotes
Final thoughts . . . 99

As soon as you take money for playing sport, it isn't sport, it's work.

Avery Brundage
Olympic athlete

1 Explain the quote in your own words. How is it connected to the topic of this unit?

2 If sport isn't work (because it isn't paid), what is Avery Brundage suggesting that it is?

3 Apart from money, what are the reasons people play sports? How many reasons can you think of?

The Inconvenient Truth of Climate Change

If you cover your eyes, you can make it go away.

CartoonStock

In this unit, you will:
- read an article about global warming.
- read an article about climate change and solutions.
- discuss opinions about climate change and global warming.

1 Critical cartoons

A Warm up

Work with a partner or in a small group. Look at the information on this page and the cartoon. Discuss the questions below.

1 What are some climate change facts you know?

2 What are the main sources of energy for your country? How much comes from oil, gas, or coal?

3 What is your country doing to help the problem of climate change?

4 What is the message of the cartoon? What is the connection to the unit topic?

> I know that climate change is ...

> I think that a lot of our energy comes from ...

> Our country is trying to fight climate change by ...

> I think the dinosaurs are like ...

MEDIA link

An Inconvenient Sequel: Truth to Power (2017) is the follow-up to the documentary *An Inconvenient Truth* by Nobel Prize-winning former vice president Al Gore. The documentary looks at the progress made to tackle climate change and Gore's work to persuade governmental leaders to invest in renewable energy.

For additional media links, go to infocus-eltseries.com

2 Core vocabulary

A Skimming and scanning

1 Find and underline the keywords in the passage. Try to guess their meanings.

Keywords

conclude	massive	pace	predict	significant
stem	substantial	tackle	thus	voter

What is Global Warming?

Global warming, or more correctly, global climate change is the name given to the rise in average temperatures around the world over the past few hundred years. Although the exact causes and effects of global warming are still a matter of debate, most scientists conclude that it is because of a substantial increase in the amount of carbon dioxide in the air. They believe this stems from the burning of fossil fuels* such as oil and coal for energy, and they predict massive changes to the world's climate.

Previously, energy needs were much less, but the invention of the car around 140 years ago changed everything. Fossil fuels are needed both to make cars and to run them. Thus, as cars became popular all over the world, there was a growing need for these fuels. The pace of growth in energy needs and in car production continues today. Some of the biggest companies in the world either make cars or produce oil.

Some people still believe that the change in global temperatures is not caused by humans. They believe there are natural explanations and that there is no significant problem. They argue that environmentalists are trying to scare voters away from governments that support big business. One thing is certain: the future holds many problems we will need to tackle.

*fossil fuel (n): an energy source such as gas and oil made in the earth from plants and animals

2 Look at the pictures below. Which picture goes best with the text above? Circle A, B, or C. Then explain your answer to a partner.

A

B

C

B Words in context: collocations

1 Look at the text on page 50. Find the keywords that form collocations with the words below.

1 scientists _____

2 _____ increase

3 _____ of growth

4 _____ problems

2 Match the four keywords with the words below to make new collocations.

1 _____ of reform

2 researchers _____

3 _____ the crisis

4 _____ amount

3 Work with a partner. Use the collocations above to make your own sentences.

1 _____

2 _____

3 _____

4 _____

C Word parts: *dict*   Example: *predict*

Words with *dict*

| contradict | dictation | dictator | diction | dictionary | predict | verdict |

1 Use the words in the box to complete the sentences below. Change the word form as necessary. Try to guess the meaning of any words you don't know.

1 The English teacher told the students to look at the _____ exercise on page 24.

2 The Mayan calendar _____ the end of the world.

3 If you don't know the meaning, look up the word in a _____.

4 The judge gave her _____ at the end of the trial.

5 I don't agree with Camila. I think the facts _____ her opinion.

6 Some countries aren't free; they are ruled by a _____.

7 Bill's perfect _____ made his speech easy to understand.

2 Work with a partner. What do you think *dict* means? Write your guess below. Then check your answer with another partner.

I think *dict* means _____.

D Discussion dictation

1 Listen and write down the questions. Then discuss them in small groups.

1 What measures _____ ?

2 What things _____ ?

3 What is _____ ?

2 Form new groups and compare your answers.

3 Reading skills

A Pre-reading

1 Quickly scan the text and circle the 10 keywords.

2 What do you think a "climate refugee" is?

3 What are two possible consequences of global warming?

B Reading

Read the text and check your answers to the pre-reading questions above. Then highlight an interesting idea in each paragraph.

Hotter and Hotter

On land and in the ocean, the average world temperature has been increasing since the nineteenth century. In many parts of the world, average temperatures are reaching historic highs. Perhaps
5 these are natural changes over time and long-term climate cycles aren't completely understood. However, most scientists conclude that this average temperature increase stems from the production of carbon dioxide by human activity.

10 Carbon dioxide is a greenhouse gas. It traps energy from the sun, thus preventing that energy from escaping into space. This is fortunate. Without carbon dioxide, we would bake by day and freeze at night. But since the nineteenth century, human activity has increased the
15 amount of carbon dioxide in the air by 40 percent. This rise is reflected in the increase in average temperatures.

We have created this problem by burning fossil fuels. These are fuels produced in the earth from plants and animals. People have always used natural products as
20 fuels. In previous eras, people used wood and coal, largely for cooking and heating, and this created carbon dioxide. But with the development of industry and the discovery of oil under the ground, the amount of carbon dioxide began to increase at a significant rate. Today,
25 as more and more countries develop, this increase is speeding up.

The result of this is that the pace of warming is also increasing. There are several reasons for this. More of

the sun's energy is retained in the atmosphere, and melting snow and ice means that less of the sun's heat 3 is reflected away. In addition, as the frozen ground in the far north warms, methane gas is released, and methane is an even stronger greenhouse gas than carbon dioxide.

If we don't stop this process, the forecast is frightening. 3 Ice fields in the far north and on high mountains will melt, and the sea level will rise. Low-lying countries such as Bangladesh will struggle with floods, and some island nations might ultimately disappear. Researchers also predict that regional rainfall patterns will change 4 and many areas of the world will become very dry. There won't be enough rainfall to produce enough food. This may lead to massive political and social problems in these areas. We might soon see "climate refugees" as people have to move from their homes to 4 find food.

The solution is plain. We have to reduce carbon dioxide levels by cutting back on our carbon footprint.* International cooperation is essential, but cooperation is difficult to achieve. Voters in developed countries want 5 to retain their standard of living, and those in poorer countries want more development in order to improve theirs. Despite the warnings of scientists, there has been no agreement to make substantial cuts so far.

The debate about how to tackle the problem goes on, 5 but meanwhile, the earth gets warmer year by year. Time is running out.

*See **4 Researching a topic** on page 54.

C Checking details

Read the questions below and circle the correct answers according to the text.

1 Which of the following statements is true?

 A People have always used oil and wood for cooking and heating.

 B The solution to global warming is obvious.

 C The release of methane gas will slow the pace of global warming.

 D Climate refugees live in Bangladesh and some island nations.

2 Which of the following statements is NOT true?

 A Carbon dioxide is useful for life on Earth.

 B Methane is a more powerful greenhouse gas than carbon dioxide.

 C The amount of carbon dioxide in the air has increased by almost half since the nineteenth century.

 D Most people who want to reduce energy use come from developing countries.

D Reference words

The words below are taken from the text. What do they refer to?

1 *These* (line 18) _____

2 *this* (line 21) _____

3 *this* (line 27) _____

4 *these* (line 44) _____

5 *those* (line 51) _____

6 *theirs* (line 53) _____

E Identifying opinions

Work with a partner and answer the questions below.

1 How would the author feel about a country that doesn't take action to reduce greenhouse gas emissions? What evidence can you find in the text to support your opinion?

2 According to the text, what do people in developing countries say when they are asked about reducing their country's production of carbon dioxide?

Discuss it

Work with a partner or in a small group. Ask and answer the questions below.

1 Look back at the ideas you highlighted. Are they the same? What are the differences?

2 Imagine the government told you that to control global warming, you could:

 - use your car only every second day, and

 - not use heaters or air conditioners at home for more than three hours a day.

 What would you feel? Could you accept it?

4 Researching a topic

A Information gathering

The carbon footprint of a product is the total amount of carbon dioxide (CO_2) and other greenhouse gases that go into the air from the time a product is made until the end of its life.

1 Work in small groups. Look at the information and discuss the questions below.

1 What factors cause the differences among the products in each table?

2 Which do you think is the most important factor?

Laundry	Carbon footprint (kg)
cold water	0.59
hot water	0.95
hot water plus clothes dryer	2.00

Car	Carbon footprint (kg)
hybrid car	44,000
small car	64,000
large car	95,000
SUV*	118,000

*Sport Utility Vehicle

Footwear	Carbon footprint (kg)
sandals	15
shoes	45
hiking boots	80

> One factor that causes a difference is ...

> I think the most important factor is probably ...

2 Work with a partner. Student A: Look at the table below. Student B: Look at the table on page 97. Ask your partner for the missing information and complete your table.

Student A

Los Angeles to New York		
Transportation	Carbon footprint (kg)	Unit
airplane	500	per seat
small car		
big SUV	1,370	per vehicle
bus		
train	120	per seat
bicycle		

B Interpreting and reporting results

Work with a new partner. Discuss the questions below.

1 Which forms of transportation are the most efficient per person?

2 Which is the least efficient? Why?

> It seems that ... produces more/less CO_2 than ...

> I'm surprised that ... is more efficient than ...

> I think this is probably because ...

5 Critical thinking

A Fact or opinion?

1 There are many different points of view on the topic of climate change. Work with a partner and decide if the following statements are fact (F) or opinion (O).

   1 Increased carbon dioxide in the atmosphere leads to an increase in average global temperature. _____

   2 Typhoons are more dangerous than rising sea levels. _____

   3 As the ice melts, sea levels will rise. _____

   4 Methane is a greenhouse gas. _____

   5 Developing countries must cut back on the use of fossil fuels. _____

2 Now write two more statements about this topic—one fact and one opinion. Then show them to another pair and ask them to say which is fact and which is opinion.

   1 _____

   2 _____

B Categorizing

1 Read these statements below. What do the speakers feel about climate change? Write 1 to 5 below (1 = not worried; 5 = very worried).

   1 "There will be a lot more natural disasters as the world climate changes. Societies will need to adapt. But we'll survive." _____

   2 "The earth's climate has often changed for natural reasons. Technology will protect us." _____

   3 "What's the problem with global warming? It has a positive effect. Ships, for example, will be able to sail from the Atlantic to the Pacific via the Canadian Arctic. That will save energy!" _____

   4 "Global warming means disaster for humans. We need to set up a central world government at the UN that must decide how much CO_2 each country can produce." _____

   5 "Until storms, hurricanes, and typhoons get really bad and more frequent, governments won't act." _____

2 Compare your answers with a partner. Explain the reasons for your choices.

C Writing

Look back at the statements in A and B above. Write a short paragraph about the different opinions on the question of global warming. Use the model below.

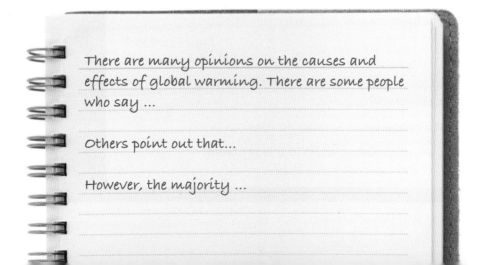

There are many opinions on the causes and effects of global warming. There are some people who say ...

Others point out that...

However, the majority ...

D Discussion

1 Work in small groups. In C, you wrote about different opinions on the question of global warming. Now read the questions below. Choose four and discuss them in your groups. Be sure to ask follow-up questions.

   1 What's the difference between global warming and climate change?

   2 Do you think humans have caused global warming?

   3 Does your country take global warming seriously? What are they doing about it?

   4 What could your country do to reduce its carbon footprint?

   5 What could you do to reduce your carbon footprint?

   6 Have you changed anything in your life because of global warming?

   7 Do you think developing countries shouldn't grow so fast?

   8 What do you think will be the result of global warming over the next 50 years?

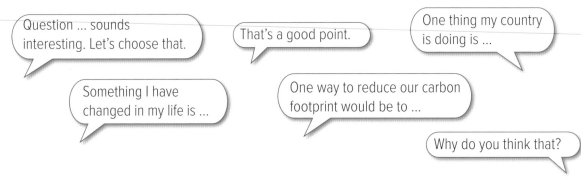

Question ... sounds interesting. Let's choose that.

That's a good point.

One thing my country is doing is ...

Something I have changed in my life is ...

One way to reduce our carbon footprint would be to ...

Why do you think that?

2 Report the results of your discussion to your classmates. The class should ask at least two follow-up questions before moving to the next group.

What do you think about ...?

Can you tell me more about that?

Do you agree that ...?

What makes you think that ...?

66 Quotable quotes
Final thoughts . . . 99

I have a feeling that climate change may be an issue as severe as a war. It may be necessary to put democracy on hold for a while.

James Lovelock
English scientist and environmentalist

1 Which is a bigger danger for society: global warming or suspending democracy?

2 Could climate change be as serious an issue as war?

3 Do you think we will find a solution to this problem?

The Global Warming Myth?

In this unit, you will:

- read an article about the meaning of *myth*.
- read an article about technological solutions to global warming.
- discuss and present your ideas about the ideal climate.

1 Critical cartoons

A Warm up

Work with a partner or in a small group. Look at the information on this page and the cartoon. Discuss the questions below.

1 What do you know about the problem of global warming?

2 Which countries will be most affected by global warming? Give examples.

3 What does the word *myth* mean? Who do you think might argue that global warming is a myth? Why?

4 What is the message of the cartoon? What is the connection to the unit topic?

> One thing I know about global warming is that ...

> I read that ... will have serious problems because ...

> I think *myth* means ...

> I think the cartoon is trying to say ...

MEDIA link

Climate Hustle (2016) is a documentary that criticizes the general scientific view about climate change. It suggests that climate change is caused more by solar activity than by human activity.

For additional media links, go to infocus-eltseries.com

2 Core vocabulary

A Skimming and scanning

1 Find and underline the keywords in the passage. Try to guess their meanings.

Keywords

acknowledge	advocate	alternative	dispute	extraordinary
flood	initial	prisoner	prospect	theory

The Meaning of Myth

The word *myth* has two general meanings. The first meaning is an ancient story in which a hero often performs an extraordinary task. An example of this is Prometheus stealing fire from the gods and giving it to humans. This angered the gods, who then made him a prisoner by chaining him to a rock. The second meaning describes a widely held belief that is not in fact true. The common feature of both meanings is the lack of scientific evidence. 5

For example, there are many myths in which the world is flooded. However, while scientists acknowledge that the stories may describe local flooding, there is just not enough water on Earth to flood all the land. If all the world's ice melted, sea levels would rise about 65 meters. This unwelcome prospect would be a major threat to people living near the sea, but the flood would still not cover all of the earth. 10

The word *myth* can be used as an insult, particularly when the dispute is over a scientific theory. When scientists are given a set of facts, they make an initial theory to best 15 explain those facts. As more facts appear, the theory may be supported or weakened. If weakened, alternative theories are made. While scientists may be strong 20 advocates of a particular theory, science depends on the facts. To call a scientific theory a myth is to say all the facts have appeared and the theory has no support. 25

2 Read the statements below. Which best summarizes the text? Circle A, B, or C. Then explain your answer to a partner.

A Scientists are no different from other people regarding their belief in myths.

B Scientists don't understand many things that happened in the past.

C Myths can refer to stories from long ago or to beliefs that aren't supported by facts.

B Words in context: collocations

1 Look at the text on page 58. Find the keywords that form collocations with the words below.

1 _____ task   **3** unwelcome _____

2 scientists _____   **4** strong _____

2 Match the four keywords with the words below to make new collocations.

1 growth _____   **5** _____ performance

2 human rights _____   **6** future _____

3 _____ ability   **7** _____ the mistakes

4 _____ the importance   **8** health _____

3 Work with a partner. Use the collocations above to make your own sentences.

1 _____

2 _____

3 _____

4 _____

C Word parts: *pro* Example: *prospect*

Words with *pro*

| produce | program | projector | prolong | propeller | prospect | provide |

1 Use the words in the box to complete the sentences below. Change the word form as necessary. Try to guess the meaning of any words you don't know.

1 The news was bad, and there was little _____ of improvement in the economy.

2 The city _____ school lunches to all children under 12.

3 This factory _____ hats.

4 The cinema operator turned down the lights, turned on the _____, and started the movie.

5 Big airplanes use jet engines, but small ones usually have _____.

6 Nick's comments _____ the meeting, so everyone missed lunch.

7 When the computer _____ crashed, all the data was lost.

2 Work with a partner. What do you think *pro* means? Write your guess below. Then check your answer with another partner.

I think *pro* means _____

D Discussion dictation

1 Listen and write down the questions. Then discuss them in small groups.

1 What unusual ___ _____ ?

2 What changes _____ ?

3 Do you _____ ?

2 Form new groups and compare your answers.

3 Reading skills

A Pre-reading

1 Quickly scan the text and circle the 10 keywords.

2 How might someone who doesn't believe humans cause global warming explain the rise in global temperatures?

3 How may some countries benefit from global warming?

B Reading

Read the text and check your answers to the pre-reading questions above. Then highlight an interesting idea in each paragraph.

 # The Myth of Global Warming?

Global warming is not a myth. It is an extraordinary problem and very serious. Some people might say it is too late to do anything about it, but that is a myth. It is a massive challenge, but we have the knowledge
5 and tools to work on it. First, we have to acknowledge the problem. Then, if we use technology and what we know in a smart way, we can lessen the harm from global warming and make our planet healthier for the future.

10 One way to help manage global warming is using renewable energy. This means getting power from the sun and wind. These methods are becoming cheaper and better. They are already changing how we get our power, and that is reducing our use of fossil fuels and
15 the amount of carbon dioxide produced.

Another hopeful prospect is a technology called carbon capture and storage (CCS). This technology takes the harmful carbon dioxide gas from power plants and factories before it is released into the
20 air. The carbon dioxide that is captured can then be stored or used in different ways. We are still in the initial stages of learning about this technology, but the first results are hopeful.

Farming also adds to global warming, but there are
25 new alternative ways of farming that are less harmful. For example, a type of farming called precision farming makes use of advanced tools like GPS and data analysis to use resources well, reduce harmful gas emissions, and grow more crops. Agroforestry,
30 which is a mix of growing trees and crops, helps to take in carbon and supports many kinds of life. These ways show us how we can use technology to create a food system that is good for the environment and fights global warming.

It is also important to take care of and fix natural areas to fight global warming. Planting more trees and fixing damaged land can take carbon dioxide from the air. Protecting wetlands and coral reefs can also help slow down the problem of floods caused by rising sea levels.

While our current ways of fighting global warming are helpful, scientists are exploring even more amazing solutions. One idea is to pull carbon dioxide right out of the air. This technology is still new, but in theory, it could greatly reduce the amount of carbon dioxide in our air. Other solutions involve making future improvements in storing energy, like new kinds of batteries. This could make renewable energy sources even more reliable.

To win the fight against global warming, we need to use technology and science, and take strong actions. The progress we have made in renewable energy, carbon capture and storage, and farming that is good for the environment, gives us hope. If we accept these current strategies and invest in future ones, we can fight global warming effectively.

It is not just about technology and science. It is also about people. Some people dispute how serious global warming is. But more and more people are starting to acknowledge that it is a real problem. Those who advocate improving the health of our planet see a brighter future. We are not prisoners of the current situation—we can change the future. Let's all rise to the challenge, knowing we have the tools to make a better tomorrow.

C Checking details

Read the questions below and circle the correct answers according to the text. (There may be more than one correct answer.)

1 Which of the following statements is true?

    A It's a myth that we can do anything about global warming.

    B The effects of global warming have worsened because of renewable energies.

    C We need to take care of natural areas to manage global warming.

    D Fossil fuels don't contribute to the problem of global warming.

2 Which of the following statements is NOT true?

    A Carbon capture technology is harmful to the planet.

    B Most people believe global warming is a problem.

    C Protecting coral reefs has a positive effect on global warming.

    D Precision farming is one cause of global warming.

D Identifying reasons

The author suggests that global warming is something that can be controlled. Four possible approaches are given. Find at least one piece of evidence in the text for each approach.

Approach	Evidence
1 Using renewable energy	
2 Use of carbon capture technology	
3 Use of precision farming	
4 Taking care of natural areas	

E Identifying opinions

Work with a partner and answer the questions below. Check (✓) the boxes. Underline any words or phrases in the text that support your choice.

1 In this text, how can the author's point of view about our ability to address global warming best be described?

    ☐ positive   ☐ neutral   ☐ negative

2 What might be the opinion of an oil company executive toward this text? Why?

    ☐ positive   ☐ neutral   ☐ negative

Discuss it

Work with a partner or in a small group. Ask and answer the questions below.

1 Look back at the ideas you highlighted. Are they the same? What are the differences?

2 Over 90 percent of scientists believe that global warming is caused by humans, but only half of Americans believe it. Why do you think this is?

3 Compare your ideas with your classmates. Which do you think are the most interesting?

4 Researching a topic

A Information gathering

1 Work in small groups. Look at the list of disaster movies below. Match each movie to the type of disaster. Then check your answers on page 97.

Movie	Type of disaster	Caused by humans?		
		Yes	No	Maybe
Contagion	climate change	☐	☐	☐
Dante's Peak	alien attack	☐	☐	☐
Don't Look Up	earthquake	☐	☐	☐
Noah	disease	☐	☐	☐
San Andreas	comet	☐	☐	☐
Terminator 3: Rise of the Machines	flood	☐	☐	☐
The Day After Tomorrow	volcano	☐	☐	☐
The Perfect Storm	hurricane/typhoon	☐	☐	☐
The Poseidon Adventure	nuclear war	☐	☐	☐
Titanic	tornado	☐	☐	☐
Twister	tsunami	☐	☐	☐
War of the Worlds	vehicle accident	☐	☐	☐

2 Which of the disasters are caused by humans? Which are caused by something else? Check (✓) the boxes in the table.

B Interpreting and reporting results

Work in small groups. Discuss the questions below.

1 Compare your results in the table. What is similar or different? Explain your reasons and give examples.

2 Why do you think most cultures have disaster movies or stories? Why do we enjoy them so much?

> We think ... could/must have been caused by ...

> People are always excited/ interested/shocked by ...

> We believe ... is clearly (not) caused by ...

> I guess watching a disaster movie or story is one way to ...

A Fact or opinion?

There are many different points of view on the topic of global warming. Work with a partner and decide if the following statements are fact (F) or opinion (O).

1   The average temperature dropped from the 1940s to the 1960s.   _____

2   Global warming has had a strong effect on population growth.   _____

3   Global warming is causing the ice caps to melt.   _____

4   All recent natural disasters are caused by global warming.   _____

5   It is a myth that reducing the use of fossil fuels will reduce carbon dioxide levels.   _____

B Categorizing

1   Decide if the following statements sound positive, neutral, or negative. Put checks (✓) in the boxes. Underline any words in the sentences that support your choice.

	Positive	Neutral	Negative
1 The media over-report global warming, and that frightens people.			
2 The world was much warmer millions of years ago.			
3 Global warming is simply part of a natural cycle.			
4 Canada and Russia will gain economically from higher global temperatures.			
5 When big companies fund global warming research, the results can't be trusted.			

2   Compare your answers with a partner. Explain the reasons for your choices.

C Writing

The graph below shows ice ages (glacials) and warmer periods between ice ages (interglacials) over the last 450,000 years. Write a short paragraph to describe the changes.

Useful verbs: *increase, climb, stay level, remain stable, decrease, fall*

Useful adjectives: *long, short, sharp, dramatic, significant, steady, gradual, slight*

If we look at the earth's temperature changes over the last 450,000 years, we see that ...

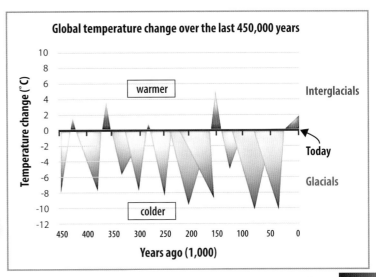

Global temperature change over the last 450,000 years

D Presentation

Work in small groups. In C, you wrote about the earth's temperature changes over time. Now you are going to discuss places in the world that have an ideal climate.

1 Discuss what makes a climate ideal in your opinion. Think about these factors:

- natural disasters (droughts, earthquakes, landslides, typhoons/hurricanes, etc.)
- temperature   • humidity   • seasons   • rainfall

2 Look at the photos below. Describe the type of climate for each place. What are the good and bad points of each climate? Which do you think is ideal? Why?

Mild (temperate)   Mediterranean   Tropical   Hot and dry

3 What other places do you know which have good climates? Explain why. Then agree on one place you think has the best climate.

4 Present your ideas to the class. Explain the reasons for your choice.

> For us, an ideal climate means ...

> Of all the places we considered, we chose ... because ...

> The factors we think are most important are ...

TIP

Posture

The way you stand is very important when presenting. It will help you look, feel, and sound confident. You should be comfortable yet alert.

DOs

- stand up straight and project your voice.
- spread your feet.
- face your audience.

DON'Ts

- lean against a desk: you will look too casual.
- move back and forth: this is distracting.

66 Quotable quotes
Final thoughts . . . 99

America has not led but fled* on the issue of global warming.

John Kerry
American politician

1 How is this quote connected to the topic of this unit?

2 The United States is often considered a leader in helping to fix problems around the world. Why is it behaving differently here? What do you think will be the result of America "fleeing" this issue?

*flee (v, past *fled*) to escape by running away

Changing Ideas of Beauty

"*This time they've totally gone too far.*"

In this unit, you will:
- read an article about beauty.
- read an article about changing ideas about beauty.
- make a presentation about beauty.

1 Critical cartoons

A Warm up

Work with a partner or in a small group. Look at the information on this page and the cartoon. Discuss the questions below.

1 Who are some top models you know of? What do they look like?

2 What makes a person attractive to you?

3 How important is beauty in your country? Give examples.

4 What is the message of the cartoon? What is the connection to the unit topic?

> Do you know ...?
> I think she's really ...

> I find people who are ... attractive.

> In my country, being beautiful is ...

> This cartoon is making the point that ...

MEDIA link

The Illusionists (2015) is a documentary that explores how global advertising and marketing industries promote beauty standards that are impossible for most people to achieve.

For additional media links, go to infocus-eltseries.com

2 Core vocabulary

A Skimming and scanning

1 Find and underline the keywords in the passage. Try to guess their meanings.

Keywords

approve	assess	asset	comparison	guard
investigation	obviously	priority	truly	virtually

 **Beauty**

There is a common saying: "Beauty is in the eye of the beholder." This means that each person (the beholder) has his or her own opinion about what is beautiful. For example, some people lie in the sun to make 5 their skin darker. Others don't approve of this exposure to the sun and wear sunscreen to guard their skin from getting dark.

In some societies, people struggle to get enough to eat, so body fat is thought to be 10 an asset. A person from those societies may find a heavier person more attractive than a thinner person. People from other societies may think differently.

However, what we call beauty may also be nature giving priority to health when choosing a mate. 15 Scientists have looked at how people assess female beauty and have found similar things among different societies. In one investigation, researchers looked at the waist-to-hip ratio: the size of the waist in comparison with the size of the hips. They found that the ideal ratio is virtually the same across cultures. The ideal for women of 0.70 is not only a sign of beauty; it also predicts good health and easy childbirth. Nature and evolution obviously also play a part in our idea of beauty. 20

So, when we say someone is truly beautiful, it expresses both our personal opinion and the influence of nature and culture.

2 Read the statements below. Which best summarizes the text? Circle A, B, or C. Then explain your answer to a partner.

A Evolution and nature influence our opinions about beauty.

B Around the world, people's idea of beauty is mostly the same.

C Everybody's opinion about beauty is different.

B Words in context: collocations

1 Look at the text on **page 66**. Find the keywords that form collocations with the words below.

1 give _____ to

2 _____ female beauty

3 _____ the same

4 _____ beautiful

2 Match the four keywords with the words below to make new collocations.

1 _____ the value

2 _____ impossible

3 _____ amazing

4 top _____

3 Work with a partner. Use the collocations above to make your own sentences.

1 _____

2 _____

3 _____

4 _____

C Word parts: *dis*   Example: *disagree*

Words with *dis*

| disadvantage | disagree | disallow | disappear | disconnect | discontinued | disrespect |

1 Use the words in the box to complete the sentences below. Change the word form as necessary. Try to guess the meaning of any words you don't know.

1 After shutting down the computer, please _____ the hard drive.

2 My favorite magazine is going to be _____; I won't be able to read it anymore.

3 The referee _____ the goal.

4 I mean no _____, but that performance wasn't your best.

5 I _____. I thought the presentation was excellent.

6 In volleyball, shorter players are at a _____.

7 Unless we protect the rainforests, thousands of animals and plants will _____.

2 Work with a partner. What do you think *dis* means? Write your guess below. Then check your answer with another partner.

I think *dis* means _____.

D Discussion dictation

1 Listen and write down the questions. Then discuss them in small groups.

1 Apart from _____?

2 Can you _____?

3 Is _____?

2 Form new groups and compare your answers.

3 Reading skills

A Pre-reading

1 Quickly scan the text and circle the 10 keywords.

2 What do women generally find attractive in men? What do men find attractive in women?

3 How was the idea of beauty 200 years ago different from today in your country?

B Reading

Read the text and check your answers to the pre-reading questions above. Then highlight an interesting idea in each paragraph.

What Is Beauty?

What do we find attractive in a person's physical appearance? Cultures differ, but there are some features that we all approve of. Women usually prefer taller men with a V-shaped upper body. Men generally
5 prefer women with a large hip-to-waist ratio and a youthful appearance. Both sexes give priority to people with features that are balanced, especially on the face.

These preferences result from human evolution. Being
10 tall and having balanced features are general signs of good health. They also suggest access to a high-quality food supply. From a male's point of view, when assessing a possible partner, a large hip-to-waist ratio and youth are assets. They indicate that a woman
15 is better able to have children. From the female evolutionary viewpoint, a tall, well-built male might be a successful hunter and guard who can feed and protect the household.

Currently, in many countries, being slim is seen as
20 attractive. Historical ideals of beauty were different. For example, if we look at European paintings from previous eras, we see that ideal figures of female beauty were extremely heavy by today's standards. The reason for this lies largely in society. What makes
25 us fat is a rich diet combined with a lack of exercise. Until a couple of hundred years ago, virtually all people lived in relative poverty. Only the rich had plenty of food and could avoid hard work. Today, the availability of high-calorie, cheap fast food in many
30 countries makes it easy for poorer people to add inches to their waistlines. In developed countries, only the rich can afford the time and money needed to exercise at sports facilities and buy high-quality healthy food.
35 Fashion also affects our ideas of what an ideal

appearance is. In recent investigations, men and women were shown pictures of women and asked to rate them in terms of attractiveness. Women in the study rated pictures of thinner women as more attractive. This shows the power of advertising in fashion. Female models are   4 usually much thinner than the average female.

We all want to be attractive, but there are negative consequences to trying to achieve beauty as defined by the fashion industry. One is eating disorders. People with an eating disorder often think that they are fat when   4 they are not fat at all. This can cause them to dangerously limit the amount of food they eat. Eating disorders were once very rare, but they have increased since the 1960s. They are common among women; young women aged between 15 and 19 make up 40 percent of new cases in   5 the US. By comparison, they are rare among men. These disorders have the highest rate of death of any mental illness.

The fashion and advertising industries are obviously to blame. Clothes are designed for and worn by thin models,   5 who are themselves often victims of eating disorders. To boost sales, food companies flood the market with fattening junk foods. At the same time, advertisers promote slimness as the ideal of beauty. It is truly time to end this unhealthy situation.   6

C Checking details

Read the questions below and circle the correct answers according to the text.

1 Which of the following statements is true?

    A Advertising is partly to blame for eating disorders.

    B Eating disorders were common in the past.

    C Eating disorders never affect men.

    D Advertisers discourage unhealthy eating habits.

2 Which of the following statements is NOT true?

    A There are common features of beauty around the world.

    B The similarity in shape and size between the left and right sides of your body is a good measure of health.

    C Being slim is a sign of attractiveness in many countries.

    D Women tend to rate thin women as less attractive than women of average weight.

D Cause and effect

The sentences below summarize the author's ideas. Each sentence follows a cause-and-effect pattern. Underline the words that represent the cause and circle the words that represent the effect.

1 A high-quality food supply often results in a tall body with balanced features.

2 Being tall with a V-shaped body is partly due to a good diet.

3 Balanced features make a person attractive to others.

4 Younger women are more likely to become mothers than older women.

5 Success in hunting depends on being tall and well built.

E Making inferences

Read the questions below and circle the correct answers according to the text. (There may be more than one correct answer.)

1 Which of the following inferences can be made from the text?

    A Attractive men and women usually belong to sports clubs.

    B Women are usually attracted to big men who like hunting.

    C Men always prefer slim women.

    D In developed countries, poor people tend to eat fast food.

2 Why were heavier women considered attractive in the past?

    A Because it showed they didn't have eating disorders.

    B Because they had a rich diet and little exercise.

    C Because it showed they were rich.

    D Because they were good workers.

Discuss it

Work with a partner or in a small group. Ask and answer the questions below.

1 Look back at the ideas you highlighted. Are they the same? What are the differences?

2 Does your culture influence your ideas of beauty? Describe ideal male and female beauty in your culture. How are they different from those in other cultures?

3 According to the text, three main influences shape our ideas of beauty. Which do you think is the most important?

4 Researching a topic

A Information gathering

1 What qualities or features make a person attractive to you? Look at the list below and add your own ideas. Then rank the qualities in order of importance to you from 1 to 10 (1 = not important; 10 = most important).

2 Now ask three classmates their opinions. Write their answers in the table.

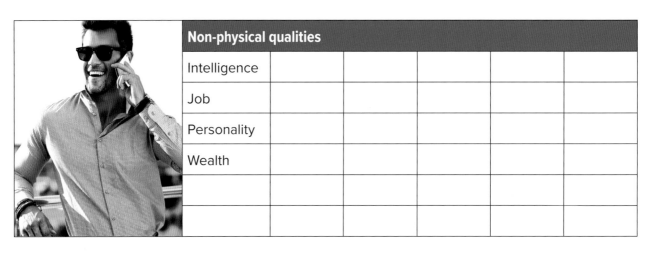

Attractiveness ranking (1–10)				
My ranking	Partner 1	Partner 2	Partner 3	Total
Physical qualities				
Age				
Body				
Face				
Non-physical qualities				
Intelligence				
Job				
Personality				
Wealth				

B Interpreting and reporting results

1 Work in small groups. Compare your rankings and add up the totals. Then report the results to the class.

2 What conclusions can you draw from your findings? Do they support the points made in the texts on pages 66 and 68?

Our results suggest that …

The majority of us think that …

It's really surprising that …

Taking into account …

When we compared our findings …

As far as I'm concerned …

5 Critical thinking

A Fact or opinion?

1 There are many different points of view on the topic of beauty. Work with a partner and decide if the following statements are fact (F) or opinion (O).

    1 Beauty is in the eye of the beholder.   _____

    2 Frank is more handsome than Pete.   _____

    3 Attractive people often have higher incomes.   _____

    4 Almost no diets result in permanent weight loss.   _____

    5 Expensive clothes make the wearer more attractive.   _____

2 Now write two more statements about this topic—one fact and one opinion. Then show them to another pair and ask them to say which is fact and which is opinion.

    1 _____

    2 _____

B Categorizing

1 Work with a partner. Decide which of the statements below the author might make. Check (✓) the box. (You can check more than one statement.)

    1 Women prefer men with good hair because it is a sign of good health.   ☐

    2 Eating disorders are less of a problem today compared with a generation ago.   ☐

    3 Having a high income is the modern equivalent of being a good hunter.   ☐

    4 Fashion has a minor influence on what people find attractive.   ☐

    5 Advertisers shouldn't be allowed to use underweight models.   ☐

2 Compare your answers with a partner. Explain the reasons for your choices.

C Writing

Write a short paragraph on the topic of beauty. Use the ideas below and think of your own conclusion.

- The fashion industry decides our ideas of beauty.
- Crazy amounts of money are spent on diets.
- Ideas of beauty change, but we live now and it's important to look good.
- It's fun to spend money on beauty products; looking attractive feels good.

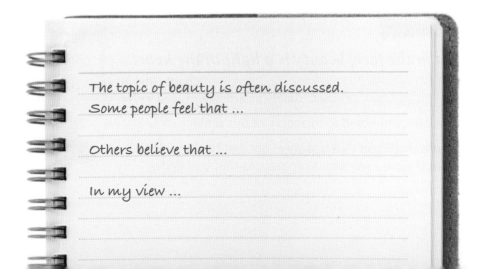

The topic of beauty is often discussed.
Some people feel that ...

Others believe that ...

In my view ...

D Presentation

1 Work in small groups. In C, you wrote about the topic of beauty and its influence. Now read the questions below. Choose four of the questions and discuss them in your groups. Be sure to ask follow-up questions.

   1 What is beauty? Is it important?

   2 Do you notice and think about beautiful things when you see them?

   3 Do your friends have the same idea of beauty as you?

   4 Do you think attractive people have an unfair advantage in life?

   5 Does the idea of beauty change in place and time? How?

   6 Who decides who or what is beautiful?

   7 Does advertising tell us what to find beautiful or not beautiful?

   8 Do you think the beauty industry is important?

2 Prepare a short presentation to the class around your answers. Discuss and choose:

   – a title for the presentation

   – who will take notes

   – two or three people who will give the presentation

Openers

Have you ever thought about … ?

A common saying about beauty is …

You may not know that …

Closers

So, to sum it up …

Let's all remember …

I'd like to end with one thought …

Openers and closers
The way you start and finish a presentation is very important. These are the parts people remember best.

Openers
This is your chance to get the audience's attention and create interest. Some ways to do this:

   • Ask a question.
   • Use a quotation.
   • State an interesting or surprising fact.

Closers
At the end of your presentation, emphasize the key points and try to leave your audience with an interesting thought. Some ways to do this:

   • Give a brief summary.
   • Give a call for action.
   • Give a personal message.
   • Show a picture or image (a visual).

3 After the presentation, the class should ask at least two follow-up questions before moving to the next group.

Quotable quotes
Final thoughts . . .

Beauty is not in the face; beauty is a light in the heart.

Khalil Gibran
Lebanese-American artist, poet, and writer

1 How is this quote connected to the topic of this unit?

2 Do you agree with Gibran that beauty is not just how you look? Why or why not? Give examples from people that you know.

Is Beauty Skin Deep?

© Guy & Rodd/Distributed by Universal Uclick via CartoonStock.com

In this unit, you will:

- read an article about changing the way we look.
- read an article about the search for beauty.
- discuss the importance of appearance in the workplace.

1 Critical cartoons

A Warm up

Work with a partner or in a small group. Look at the information on this page and the cartoon. Discuss the questions below.

1 What are some of the most common ways people can improve their appearance?

2 What is considered beautiful in TV, movies, and on social media today?

3 Besides beauty, what are some reasons people make changes to their bodies? Give examples.

4 Why is the cartoon funny? What is the connection to the unit topic?

> One way that people try to improve their appearance is ...

> I think most people consider beauty as ...

> A lot of people change ... because they want to ...

> What makes this cartoon funny is ...

 **MEDIA link**

Take My Nose ... Please! (2017) is a film that looks at the pressures on women to maintain their youth and beauty. Two female comedians discuss surgery and their fears of aging.

For additional media links, go to infocus-eltseries.com

2 Core vocabulary

A Skimming and scanning

1 Find and underline the keywords in the passage. Try to guess their meanings.

Keywords

| context | elsewhere | equipment | pose | procedure |
| prompt | represent | restore | surgery | urge |

Improving on Nature?

How we change what nature gives us can tell us a lot about ourselves. Some procedures to change our natural selves are so common we hardly think of them. For example, we wear glasses or contact lenses to improve how we see. Others aren't as common, especially those concerning our appearance. Some people aren't satisfied with their looks, and this prompts them to take action. What changes they make may depend on their culture. In some countries, people use only makeup and color to change their looks. In other places, such as Polynesia, tattoos are popular. Elsewhere, people may go to hospitals, which use special equipment to carry out cosmetic surgery.

5

10

We change ourselves in many ways and for different reasons. One reason is that the changes represent a certain lifestyle a person has chosen. The decision to change one's looks can also be seen within the context of a person's career. For example, actors who undergo surgery to restore their youthful looks can make their careers last longer and increase their income. Is that so different from wanting to do more by wearing glasses? While the urge to change one's face with cosmetic surgery may seem strange to some people, there may be good reasons for doing so. Researchers have found that people form first impressions within 10 seconds of meeting another person. This poses problems for people who lack confidence in their appearance.

15

20

2 Read the statements below. Which best summarizes the text? Circle A, B, or C. Then explain your answer to a partner.

A Cosmetic surgery is used to improve people's looks in some countries.

B There are many reasons for changing our physical appearance.

C Doctors are able to suggest many improvements to how we look.

B Words in context: collocations

1 Look at the text on page 74. Find the keywords that form collocations with the words below.

1 common _____

2 _____ (someone) to take action

3 cosmetic _____

4 _____ to change

5 _____ problems

2 Match the five keywords with the words below to make new collocations.

1 _____ a response

2 _____ a threat

3 heart _____

4 to follow a _____

5 strong _____

6 _____ a challenge

7 complicated _____

8 knee _____

9 _____ a review of the rules

10 sudden _____

3 Work with a partner. Use the collocations above to make your own sentences.

1 _____

2 _____

3 _____

4 _____

5 _____

C Word parts: *poly*   Example: *Polynesia*

Words with *poly*

| polyester   polygamy   polyglot   polygon   Polynesia   polysyllabic   polytechnic |

1 Use the words in the box to complete the sentences below. Try to guess the meaning of any words you don't know.

1 Monica is a _____—she speaks 10 languages.

2 This shirt is made of a blend of cotton and _____.

3 Tahiti is one of the main islands in _____.

4 Hee-sun studied nutrition at a local _____.

5 A square is a four-sided _____.

6 _____ is illegal in most countries.

7 Banana is a _____ word.

2 Work with a partner. What do you think *poly* means? Write your guess below. Then check your answer with another partner.

I think *poly* means _____.

D Discussion dictation

1 Listen and write down the questions. Then discuss them in small groups.

1 What are _____?

2 What things _____?

3 Would you _____?

2 Form new groups and compare your answers.

A Pre-reading

1 Quickly scan the text and circle the 10 keywords.

2 Where does the word *tattoo* come from?

3 What are the main reasons why people have plastic surgery?

B Reading

Read the text and check your answers to the pre-reading questions above. Then highlight an interesting idea in each paragraph.

The Never-Ending Desire for Beauty

Humans have always tried to change and improve the way they look. We see this not only in changing fashions in clothes and hairstyles, but also in more lasting actions such as tattooing, body piercing, and
5 cosmetic surgery.

Tattooing is the procedure of putting ink under the skin with a needle in order to make a design or picture. People refer to this type of art as their "ink." The word *tattoo* comes from the Tahitian word tatau.
10 It entered English following the historic voyages of Captain Cook to Polynesia in the eighteenth century, where people commonly had tattoos on their bodies and faces. Tattooing has been practiced there and elsewhere over long periods. A frozen body found
15 on the border between Austria and Italy from 5,300 years ago had multiple tattoos. They have been found on mummies from Egypt, too. Until the modern era, tattoos weren't common in the West. However, over the last 30 years, they have become a popular form
20 of expression among young people. And the spread of removable tattoos means that they no longer need to be permanent. People acquire tattoos for many reasons. Some may mark an important event in a person's
25 life such as a birth or death. Others represent love. Many are simply for looks—the beauty of the artwork.

In a similar way to tattooing,
30 body piercing is also growing more and more popular among young people. Common places for piercings are the lips, tongue, and ears.
35 Some people even have

objects put under the skin of their foreheads to make them look as if they have horns. A recent survey found that 19 percent of adults in the US had pierced tongues. As with tattooing, body piercing isn't new—many cultures have such traditions, in particular piercing of the ears, nose, and lips.

The current popularity of tattooing and body piercing represents the basic desire to improve one's looks. The growth of plastic surgery using modern medical techniques needs to be seen in this context. Plastic surgery refers to surgical procedures that repair, restore, or improve damaged body parts. During World War I, the need to treat the awful wounds suffered by soldiers prompted doctors to develop anesthesia, surgical equipment, and new drugs. These advances made modern plastic surgery possible.

Plastic surgery may still be needed following an accident or disease, but often it is done just to change the way a person looks. Today, people globally spend around US$67 billion annually on surgery to make themselves look better. The most common operations are those that change the shape and size of the nose, eyes, and breasts.

Critics say these procedures pose risks and they urge people to avoid them. They suggest that a doctor's time could be better spent treating sick people. However, these critics don't understand human nature. They forget the happiness and confidence that may come from a person's cosmetic surgery. Given the universal human wish to appear attractive, such procedures are truly here to stay.

C Checking details

Read the questions below and circle the correct answers according to the text.

1 Which of the following statements is true?

   A Tattooing is a form of cosmetic surgery.
   B Tattoo is the Polynesian name for the island of Tahiti.
   C Plastic surgery began to develop because of World War II injuries.
   D Critics believe doctors shouldn't waste time on plastic surgery.

2 Which of the following statements is NOT true?

   A In all human history, people have changed their appearance for fashion.
   B Almost one half of people in the US have tongue piercings.
   C Cosmetic surgery is one kind of plastic surgery.
   D Most cosmetic surgery involves the nose, eyes, and breasts.

D Cause and effect

Work with a partner. Five of the sentences below represent causes and five represent effects. Draw an arrow from the cause to the effect in each case.

1 Doctors developed modern plastic surgery.
2 People want to remember an important life event.
3 Cosmetic surgery can be risky.
4 People put objects under their skin.
5 Cosmetic surgery will always be with us.

A People appear to have horns.
B Soldiers were wounded in war.
C People should avoid cosmetic surgery.
D There is a universal desire to be attractive.
E People get a tattoo.

E Making inferences

Read the statements below and circle the correct answers according to the text. (There may be more than one correct answer.)

1 This supports the evidence that the human desire to improve appearance is universal.

   A Tattooing is an ancient Asian art that is now popular in the West.
   B Many people do body piercing because it is fashionable.
   C Tattooing is just a trend that will soon disappear.
   D Surgery to help improve the appearance of damaged body parts is possible because of advances in medicine.

2 The author's opinion about people changing their physical appearance is that …

   A it is a basic human desire that won't disappear.
   B doctors shouldn't waste their time on such procedures.
   C it is much too expensive.
   D it can make people happier.

Discuss it

Work with a partner or in a small group. Ask and answer the questions below.

1 Look back at the ideas you highlighted. Are they the same? What are the differences?

2 If you could have a tattoo or a body piercing for just one week, what would you choose? Describe it.

3 Should people with tattoos be banned from doing some jobs? Which ones? Why?

4 Researching a topic

A Information gathering

Interview three people for their opinions on each of the statements below. Write their names and grade their opinions 1 to 5 in the table below (1 = they strongly agree; 5 = they strongly disagree).

Opinion statement	Name:					Name:					Name:				
	1	2	3	4	5	1	2	3	4	5	1	2	3	4	5
1 Boyfriends should be taller than their girlfriends.															
2 Eyelid surgery makes eyes look more beautiful.															
3 Men look better in business suits.															
4 After age 45, women shouldn't wear red lipstick.															
5 Overweight doctors can't be trusted.															
6 TV news reporters should be good looking.															

B Interpreting and reporting results

1 **Work in small groups. Discuss the questions below.**

   1 Compare your answers in the above table. What are the similarities and differences?

   2 Which statements does your group agree and disagree with the most? Why?

2 **Discuss with the class.**

   1 Choose one of the statements and report the views of your group to your classmates.

   2 Which statements does the class agree and disagree with the most? Why?

We strongly agree that ...

Most of us didn't think that ...

None of us agreed that ...

We don't think it matters ...

We didn't have a strong opinion about ...

We agree/disagree the most with the statement ... because ...

Critical thinking

A Fact or opinion?

1 There are many different points of view on the topic of beauty and physical appearance. Work with a partner and decide if the following statements are fact (F) or opinion (O).

1 Piercing one's nose can lead to infection. _____

2 Real beauty lies in a person's character. _____

3 Doctors should treat the sick rather than try to make people beautiful. _____

4 Cosmetic surgery is rare in poorer countries. _____

5 Tattoos are an expression of a person's character. _____

2 Now write two more statements about this topic—one fact and one opinion. Then show them to another pair and ask them to say which is fact and which is opinion.

1 _____

2 _____

B Categorizing

1 Decide if the following statements sound positive, neutral, or negative. Put checks (✓) in the boxes. Underline any words in the sentences that support your choice.

	Positive	Neutral	Negative
1 Tattoos are a beautiful form of self-expression.			
2 Cosmetic surgery is unnecessary and risky.			
3 Body piercing is an ancient practice.			
4 Plastic surgery really began in World War I.			
5 Most people care about their appearance too much.			

2 Compare your answers with a partner. Explain the reasons for your choices.

C Writing

Look back at the statements in A and B above. Write a short paragraph about the positive and negative consequences of altering one's appearance. Use the model below.

There are various reasons why cosmetic surgery is becoming more and more popular. First, …

In addition, …

However, there are also some dangers. For example, …

Personally, I …

D Discussion

Work in small groups. Discuss the questions below.

1 Is there an expected appearance for how people in different professions look?

2 Look at the people below and try to guess their professions. Discuss and list the reasons for your guesses.

A

B

C

D

E

F

> I think we expect people who work as ... to look ...

> I think he/she looks like a ... because ...

> My guess is that he/she is probably ...

> I think he/she looks too ... to be ...

3 How important is appearance in the professional world in your country? What would you think if your doctor wore a T-shirt or your teacher wore an expensive Italian suit?

> I would/wouldn't mind if my doctor ...

> I think it's really important for ... to ...

Quotable quotes
Final thoughts . . .

Sometimes I bust out and do things so permanent. Like tattoos and marriage.

Drew Barrymore
American actor

1 Drew Barrymore has been married a number of times and has several tattoos. What do you think she means?

2 Besides tattoos and marriage, what other things do people do that are "permanent"?

3 Should marriage be for life?

Vegetarianism

AN EARLY VEGETARIAN
RETURNING FROM A KILL

In this unit, you will:
- read an article about a plant-based diet.
- read an article about the reasons for choosing a plant-based diet.
- discuss ideas about vegetarianism.

1 Critical cartoons

A Warm up

Work with a partner or in a small group. Look at the information on this page and the cartoon. Discuss the questions below.

1 Do you eat meat? Are there any animals or animal parts that you wouldn't eat? Why?

2 Studies show that vegetarians live about seven years longer than meat eaters. Why do you think this is so?

3 What are some of the reasons people become vegetarians?

4 What makes the cartoon interesting? What is the connection to the unit topic?

> I eat meat, but I would never eat ... because ...

> One reason why vegetarians live longer is ...

> Some people become vegetarians because ...

> This cartoon is interesting because ...

MEDIA link

What the Health (2017) is a documentary that looks at the effects that industrial animal foods have on our personal health and the general community.

For additional media links, go to infocus-eltseries.com

A Skimming and scanning

1 Find and underline the keywords in the passage. Try to guess their meanings.

Keywords

appropriate	capture	crops	declare	decline
eliminate	pursue	religious	requirement	threaten

A Vegetable Diet

People become vegetarians for very different reasons. Some stop eating meat for health reasons. For some, it may be religious—they believe eating meat goes against the wishes of their gods. Other people decline to eat meat for moral reasons. They declare that "meat is murder." They believe that it isn't appropriate to kill animals for any reason. Sometimes, they
5   pursue people who wear fur coats and throw paint on them. Finally, others think that if we stop eating meat, we will eliminate many of the problems caused by industrial farms. These farms treat plants or animals like industrial products. Unlike traditional farms, they usually raise only one type of animal or grow only one or two crops, like corn and soybean. They use many kilograms of chemicals to make their products grow more quickly.

10   For most vegetarians, nature is divided into plants and animals. They believe that animals have more rights than plants. This is unlike traditional farmers, who believe that all living things are important. For example, a grassland farmer knows that grasslands are healthiest when they are in balance. Grasslands need a variety of grasses to capture the sunlight. They need animals to eat the grasses and they need meat-eating animals, like humans, to eat the
15   grass eaters. Each is a requirement for a healthy system.

But vegetarians and industrial farmers focus on a single part of the natural cycle. Because of this, it is clear to this author that both threaten the balance of nature.

2 Read the titles below. Which would also be a good title for the text? Circle A, B, or C. Then explain your answer to a partner.

A   The Benefits of Vegetarianism
B   What Vegetarians Believe
C   The Problems of Industrial Farming

B Words in context: collocations

1 Look at the text on **page 82**. Find the keywords that form collocations with the words below.

1 _____ meat   **3** _____ problems

2 _____ people   **4** grow _____

2 Match the four keywords with the words below to make new collocations.

1 _____ an invitation   **5** _____ goals

2 _____ ripen   **6** _____ fail

3 _____ to comment   **7** _____ a career

4 _____ waste   **8** _____ the need

3 Work with a partner. Use the collocations above to make your own sentences.

1 _____

2 _____

3 _____

4 _____

C Word parts: *kilo*   Example: *kilogram*

Words with *kilo*

| kilobyte | kilocalorie | kilogram | kilohertz | kilometer | kiloton | kilowatt |

1 Use the words in the box to complete the sentences below. Change the word form as necessary.

1 A liter of water weighs 1 _____.

2 A mile is approximately 1.6 _____.

3 That electric heater is rated at 2 _____.

4 Tanya burned 400 _____ by running up the hill three times.

5 Text files are quite small; they take up only a few _____ on your hard drive.

6 Young people can hear a range of sounds up to 20 _____.

7 Nuclear explosions are measured in _____.

2 Work with a partner. What do you think *kilo* means? Write your guess below. Then check your answer with another partner.

I think *kilo* means _____.

D Discussion dictation

1 Listen and write down the questions. Then discuss them in small groups.

1 Do you _____ ?

2 What are _____ ?

3 Would people _____ ?

2 Form new groups and compare your answers.

A Pre-reading

1 Quickly scan the text and circle the 10 keywords.

2 How many reasons can you think of for becoming a vegetarian?

3 Does eating a lot of meat carry any health risks? What are they?

B Reading

Read the text and check your answers to the pre-reading questions above. Then highlight an interesting idea in each paragraph.

Vegetarianism:
The Healthy and Moral Choice

What is a vegetarian? It seems like a simple question, but the answer is complicated because many people who follow very different diets all declare themselves vegetarians. Some, known as vegans, eat no animal products at all: no meat, no fish, no eggs, no products made from milk such as butter and cheese, and no honey. Some vegans, known as fruitarians, go even further. They avoid killing plants, eating only fruit, seeds, beans, and nuts. Other vegetarians are less extreme, eating no products that require killing animals. They decline to eat meat or fish but do eat milk products and eggs. Finally, there are vegetarians who eat some kinds of meat and fish. Some eat fish but no meat; some eat fish and chicken but no red meat such as beef. Because such people eat fish or chicken, strict vegetarians don't consider them to be vegetarians at all.

There are multiple good reasons for becoming a vegetarian. First, animals raised for food are kept in cruel conditions, where they suffer and are ultimately killed. It is simply wrong to cause the death and suffering of another living creature. With their religious beliefs, Hindus and Buddhists share this point of view. As well, it is wrong to use land to raise animals for their meat. Why? The amount of land and energy required to produce a kilogram of meat protein is about 10 times that needed to produce the equivalent amount of plant protein. Switching to a non-meat diet means more people could be fed on the same amount of land. In a world where almost 10 percent of the population struggles in extreme poverty, a non-meat diet is fairer and more appropriate.

Apart from moral reasons, the current method of raising animals in massive factory farms threatens the environment. These farms not only contribute to pollution and disease in rural areas but also to climate change in several ways. First, cattle are a source of methane, a gas that has a much more significant greenhouse warming effect than carbon dioxide (CO_2). As they digest food, cattle produce around 18 percent of the methane in the atmosphere. In addition, tropical rainforest is burned and cut down in order to grow crops to feed cattle. This adds CO_2 to the atmosphere and means there is no forest to capture CO_2 and produce oxygen. Furthermore, producing animal protein uses a lot of energy, because of its requirement of oil-based chemicals and fuel. In all these ways, our hunger for cheap meat adds to the global warming problem.

Finally, we should all pursue a vegetarian diet for health reasons. A diet rich in meat is also often one that is high in fat. This can lead to disease, especially heart disease and cancer. On average, vegetarians live several years longer than meat eaters. Eliminating meat from our food will enable us to lead a healthier and longer life.

C Checking details

Read the questions below and circle the correct answers according to the text.

1   Which of the following statements is true?
   A   In the same field, more plant protein can be grown than meat protein.
   B   Factory farms don't cause pollution.
   C   Cattle farming decreases the amount of greenhouse gas in the air.
   D   A diet that includes a lot of vegetables probably also has a lot of fat.

2   Which of the following statements is NOT true?
   A   Vegans eat no animal products.
   B   Some vegetarians eat eggs.
   C   Some Hindus eat meat for religious reasons.
   D   Some people object to the conditions used for raising animals for food.

D Identifying reasons

Three people explain why they are vegetarians below. Fill in each blank with one word that describes their reasons. Then identify the paragraph that best fits each situation.

Paragraph

1   "Last month my best friend Dan's father died. I was shocked because he was only 50 years old. He loved meat and had a big appetite. I guess I gave up meat for _____ reasons."   _____

2   "Every day, tropical rainforests are cut down to use the land to grow soybeans. The beans are then fed to beef cattle. I quit eating meat for _____ reasons."   _____

3   "I believe all life is precious. I couldn't kill an animal, and I believe if you can't kill animals, you shouldn't eat them. I'm a vegan for _____ reasons."   _____

E Making inferences

Read the questions below and circle the correct answers according to the text. (There may be more than one correct answer.)

1   Some vegetarians avoid honey because ...
   A   they think honey contains a lot of fat.
   B   they object to using any animal to produce food.
   C   their religion instructs them not to eat it.
   D   they think it is wrong to cause the death of another living being.

2   Other than moral reasons, what are some reasons people might give for being vegetarians?
   A   It will help eliminate hunger in the world.
   B   Tropical rainforest can be used for farming.
   C   They will live longer.
   D   The production of methane gas will increase.

Discuss it

Work with a partner or in a small group. Ask and answer the questions below.

1   Look back at the ideas you highlighted. Are they the same? What are the differences?

2   If you were cooking a vegetarian meal for some friends, what would you cook and why?

3   Would you marry a vegetarian if it meant you couldn't cook meat at home?

4 Researching a topic

A Information gathering

Work with a partner. Ask how many meals he or she had over the past few days, and how many meals contained meat. Complete the table below. Then work out the total number of meals and the percentage of meals with meat.

Meal	Breakfast		Lunch		Dinner		Snacks	
	Yes/No	Meat?	Yes/No	Meat?	Yes/No	Meat?	Yes/No	Meat?
Today								
Yesterday								
Two days ago								
Total								

Total number of meals: _____   Total number of meals with meat: _____ = _____%

B Interpreting and reporting results

1 Share your results with the class. Find out the class percentage of meals eaten with meat in them. Is your partner above or below the average?

2 The chart below shows the consumption of meat around the world. Discuss the data with your classmates. Do any figures surprise you?

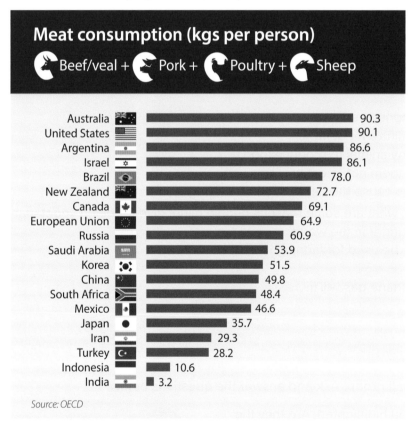

Meat consumption (kgs per person)
Beef/veal + Pork + Poultry + Sheep

Australia	90.3
United States	90.1
Argentina	86.6
Israel	86.1
Brazil	78.0
New Zealand	72.7
Canada	69.1
European Union	64.9
Russia	60.9
Saudi Arabia	53.9
Korea	51.5
China	49.8
South Africa	48.4
Mexico	46.6
Japan	35.7
Iran	29.3
Turkey	28.2
Indonesia	10.6
India	3.2

Source: OECD

I never thought that ...

I didn't expect to find that ...

It surprises me that ...

It's interesting to compare ...

The figures show that ...

5 Critical thinking

A Fact or opinion?

There are many different points of view on the topic of vegetarianism. Work with a partner and decide if the following statements are fact (F) or opinion (O).

1 Some vegetarians avoid meat for religious reasons.   _____

2 Killing animals for food is immoral.   _____

3 Eating animal products contributes to climate change.   _____

4 A vegetarian diet is healthier than one that includes meat.   _____

5 Vegetarians are kinder than meat eaters.   _____

B Categorizing

1 Decide if the following statements sound positive, negative, or neutral. Put checks (✓) in the boxes. Underline any words in the sentences that support your choice.

	Positive	Neutral	Negative
1 There are many different kinds of vegetarians.			
2 With a plant-based diet, more people can be fed on the same amount of land.			
3 Factory farming causes global warming.			
4 Many Buddhists and Hindus are vegetarians.			
5 A diet rich in meat is often high in fat.			

2 Compare your answers with a partner. Explain the reasons for your choices.

C Writing

What are other positive or negative opinions about vegetarianism? Look at pictures A–D below and write a positive or a negative statement about each one. You may want to look back at the texts on pages 82 and 84.

A
B
C
D

Picture A:

Picture B:

Picture C:

Picture D:

D Discussion

1 Work in small groups. In C, you wrote about positive and negative opinions about vegetarianism. Now read the statements below from Daniel, a beef cattle farmer. Discuss each statement in your groups. What new arguments does Daniel bring to the discussion? Do you agree or disagree with him? Be sure to share your opinions and ask follow-up questions.

I think people need meat to stay strong and healthy.

I can't imagine a meal without meat. It's delicious and satisfying.

Life is short. Why not enjoy good things like great steaks and fine wines?

Meat production gives jobs to many people. We shouldn't worry about animals.

My family has been raising beef on the same farm for over 100 years with no environmental problems.

Vegetarians must believe animals are as important as people. That's crazy.

2 Report the results of your discussion to the class. How many of your classmates agree with Daniel? How many think vegetarianism is a good thing?

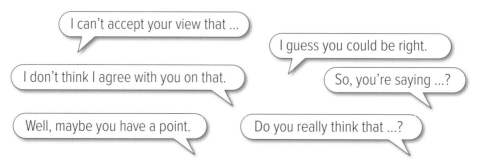

I can't accept your view that ...

I guess you could be right.

I don't think I agree with you on that.

So, you're saying ...?

Well, maybe you have a point.

Do you really think that ...?

Quotable quotes
Final thoughts . . .

To my mind, the life of a lamb is no less precious than that of a human being. I should be unwilling to take the life of a lamb for the sake of the human body.

Mahatma Gandhi
Indian lawyer and politician

1 What is Mahatma Gandhi famous for? Did you know he was a vegetarian?

2 How is this quote connected to the topic of this unit?

3 Do you agree or disagree with Gandhi? Do you believe that an animal's life is as valuable as a person's life?

MEAT SHOPPE
ANY FRESHER AND IT WOULD HEAL

SPECIAL

BALDWIN

"I dunno. Maybe we need a new slogan."

In this unit, you will:
- read an article about the history of using animals.
- read an article about factory farming.
- discuss the use of animals by humans.

1 Critical cartoons

A Warm up

Work with a partner or in a small group. Look at the information on this page and the cartoon. Discuss the questions below.

1 For what kind of foods is freshness important?

2 What kinds of meats get the highest prices? Why?

3 What things do companies do to produce meat quickly and cheaply?

4 What is the message of the cartoon? What is the connection to the unit topic?

> I think freshness is important for ...

> One really expensive meat is ...

> One thing companies do is ...

> The cartoon makes you think about ...

MEDIA link

Dominion (2018) is an Australian documentary that uses drones and hidden cameras to expose the dark side of modern animal agriculture. It questions how humans rule the animal kingdom.

For additional media links, go to infocus-eltseries.com

A Skimming and scanning

1 Find and underline the keywords in the passage. Try to guess their meanings.

Keywords

abuse	alongside	circumstance	complaint	investment
purchase	shareholder	sort	strategy	vehicle

Meat Made Man

When people walk into their local store, they don't think about the history of food. As they take out their money to purchase their food, their only complaint might be the price. They don't realize that food has never been this cheap or easily available.

Some people have strong feelings about meat. They complain about animal abuse.
5 However, they are probably not aware how eating meat has changed humans. Many thousands of years ago, humans ate all sorts of animals, but it was the discovery of fire that changed everything. This is because cooked meat is one of the best foods for humans. No one knows the circumstances surrounding this discovery, but one thing is certain: it helped humans become bigger, stronger, and faster. That's not all. In order to
10 catch large animals, which are harder to hunt, humans had to work alongside each other, learn to communicate, and develop strategies to kill the big animals. This investment of time and energy paid off with more food.

Much later, people realized they could keep animals for work or food. They used animals to pull vehicles and transport food to other people, and this helped cities grow. Our
15 use of animals continues today. In developed countries, much of our food comes from factory farms run by large businesses. Company profits keep shareholders happy while low prices keep customers happy. From the beginning of civilization up to modern businesses, we owe much to the animals we keep and eat.

2 Look at the pictures below. Which picture goes best with the text above? Circle A, B, or C. Then explain your answer to a partner.

A

B

C

B Words in context: collocations

1 Look at the text on page 90. Find the keywords that form collocations with the words below.

1 _____ food

2 animal _____

3 _____ surrounding

4 develop _____

5 _____ of time

2 Match the five keywords with the words below to make new collocations.

1 _____ of power

2 financial _____

3 _____ goods

4 marketing _____

5 under the _____

6 value of the _____

7 difficult _____

8 drug _____

9 _____ online

10 management _____

3 Work with a partner. Use the collocations above to make your own sentences.

1 _____

2 _____

3 _____

4 _____

5 _____

C Word parts: *ab*   Example: *abuse*

Words with *ab*

| abduct | abnormal | absent | absolute | abstain | abstract | abuse |

1 Use the words in the box to complete the sentences below. Change the word form as necessary. Try to guess the meaning of any words you don't know.

1 The neighbors were arrested for child _____.

2 It was freezing yesterday and hot today. This sure is _____ weather.

3 Sajid thinks he was _____ by aliens.

4 Maria was _____ from class today.

5 Rob's doctor told him to _____ from alcohol.

6 The museum has many _____ paintings.

7 Hundreds of years ago, kings and queens had _____ power.

2 Work with a partner. What do you think *ab* means? Write your guess below. Then check your answer with another partner.

I think *ab* means _____.

D Discussion dictation

1 Listen and write down the questions. Then discuss them in small groups.

1 What are _____ ?

2 Do you think _____ ?

3 What do you think _____ ?

2 Form new groups and compare your answers.

3 Reading skills

A Pre-reading

1 Quickly scan the text and circle the 10 keywords.

2 Why do we keep some animals for food but not others? Think of at least two reasons.

3 Try to imagine the life of an animal raised for food on a modern farm. How do you think that animal's life is different from 100 years ago?

B Reading

Read the text and check your answers to the pre-reading questions above. Then highlight an interesting idea in each paragraph.

Animal Slaves

Once, there were no farms. All humans were hunter-gatherers. We hunted wild animals and collected wild food such as fruit and nuts. We moved from place to place and developed strategies for hunting
5 animals and looking for plants we could eat. Then, approximately 10,000 years ago, people discovered that they could grow crops and keep certain animals to use for food or for work. Thus began farming.

Adapting animals for use as food or for work such
10 as pulling vehicles is called "domestication." The first animals to be domesticated were dogs; these were followed by sheep, pigs, goats, and cows. Some animals, for example rabbits, weren't domesticated until the modern era. In the book *Guns, Germs, and*
15 *Steel*, author Jared Diamond discusses which sorts of animals can be domesticated. First, he suggests, they must be able to eat a broad diet, and it is especially useful if they don't consume the food humans eat. They must also have a fast growth rate. Slow-growing
20 animals need too much care before they reach a useful size. Next, they must be able to be bred in captivity*. Some animals, such as the panda, are difficult to breed in captivity. In addition, they must be able to live alongside humans and not be aggressive.
25 Lions and hyenas are clearly not suitable for this reason.

As more and more animals were domesticated over time, farms developed. Animals were captive, but how they lived was mostly unchanged from the wild
30 state. Domesticated cattle in a field eating grass are basically the same as a group of wild cattle doing the same thing. This is still the picture most of us see in our minds when we think of a farm: contented animals chewing fresh, green grass in wide, open fields.

However, circumstances have changed, and most modern 3 farms are very different. In the second half of the twentieth century, the demand for cheap food and the pressure from shareholders to make a profit from their investments led to the factory farm. The life for farm animals at this kind of facility is not good—animal welfare is not a priority, 4 and they often suffer in terrible conditions. Unfortunately, this treatment continues when the animals are killed. Again, profit rules, and speed is the key to profit. Because workers have to kill as quickly as possible, mistakes are made. Some animals are still alive after their throats are 4 cut, and they are boiled or skinned alive.

All of this takes place behind closed doors, and the public is largely unaware of the circumstances under which the killing takes place. We go to the supermarket and purchase our cheap food. Perhaps we notice the 5 traditional farm pictured on the label. Usually, we think no more about it. But if we did know how these animals suffer from this abuse, would we make a complaint and change our eating habits? Would we give up cheap food to ensure proper treatment of farm animals? Would you? 5

captivity (n): when an animal is kept in a zoo or a person is kept as a prisoner, rather than being free

C Checking details

Read the questions below and circle the correct answers according to the text.

1 Which of the following statements is true?

    A Factory farms usually make sure animals have plenty of space to live.
    B Farm animals are usually easy to look after but slow growing.
    C Cows were domesticated before sheep.
    D Factory farms are more interested in their shareholders than the treatment of animals.

2 Which of the following statements is NOT true?

    A Farming began approximately 10,000 years ago.
    B Many people know little about the condition of animals in factory farms.
    C Domestic animals can't usually eat a wide range of foods.
    D Modern farms and traditional farms are very different.

D Identifying reasons

Work with a partner. Find a reason in the text for each farming development listed below.

Development	Reason
1 Birth of farming	_____
2 Domestication of cows	_____
3 Growth of factory farms	_____
4 Fast killing of animals	_____
5 People unaware of how animals were treated	_____

E Making inferences

Read the statements below and circle the correct answers according to the text. (There may be more than one correct answer.)

1 The greatest effect of the birth of farming was to allow people to …

    A stop moving and settle in one area.
    B begin using animals for transportation.
    C change the way animals live and die.
    D develop new ways to make products.

2 Modern farming techniques …

    A usually keep animals indoors rather than allow them to go outside.
    B protect people by locking up dangerous animals.
    C often cause animals much suffering and pain.
    D are usually open for the public to see.

Discuss it

Work with a partner or in a small group. Ask and answer the questions below.

1 Look back at the ideas you highlighted. Are they the same? What are the differences?

2 How did people live before there were any farms or domesticated animals? How did they find food?

3 If people watched factory farming and meat processing, how do you think they would react? How would you react?

4 Researching a topic

A Information gathering

1 Make a list of the different things animals are used for in the table below. The photos give you some ideas. Then write down the types of animal used for each purpose in column A.

Animals and their uses		
Use	Type of animal	
	A: Your ideas	B: Your partner's ideas

2 Work with a partner. Compare your ideas. Make notes in column B.

B Interpreting and reporting results

1 Work in small groups. Discuss the questions below.

   1 How are your lists similar? How are they different?

   2 Which uses are most popular in your country? How has this changed in the last 100 years?

   3 In which ways are animals part of your life? Which animals?

   4 What do you think would happen to the animals listed if people stopped using them?

2 Now report your group's most interesting results to the class.

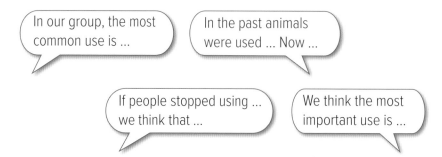

In our group, the most common use is ...

In the past animals were used ... Now ...

If people stopped using ... we think that ...

We think the most important use is ...

Critical thinking

A Fact or opinion?

There are many different points of view on the topic of the use of animals by humans. Work with a partner and decide if the following statements are fact (F) or opinion (O).

1 Humans don't have the right to kill animals for food. _____

2 Dogs were domesticated before other animals. _____

3 Testing cosmetics on animals is necessary to protect humans. _____

4 All farm animals today are treated badly. _____

5 Factory farms began sometime after 1950. _____

B Categorizing

1 Decide if the following statements sound positive, neutral, or negative. Put checks (✓) in the boxes. Underline any words in the sentences that support your choice.

	Positive	Neutral	Negative
1 Good food has never been so cheap.			
2 We are smarter because humans ate meat long ago.			
3 Buying fur coats supports suffering and cruelty.			
4 Farm animals are so stressed they become sick and need antibiotics.			
5 Factory farms were created mainly because of the demand for cheap food.			

2 Compare your answers with a partner. Explain the reasons for your choices.

C Writing

Look back at the statements in A and B above. Write a short paragraph about the arguments for and against using animals. Use the model below.

> People often hold strong opinions about using animals for food or other purposes. Those who are in favor of … say …
>
> As well, …
>
> However, their opponents claim that …
>
> In addition, …
>
> There will probably never be an end to this discussion since …

D Discussion

Work in groups. In C, you wrote about the arguments for and against the use of animals by humans. Now you are going to consider some related issues.

1 Read the questions below. Choose three and discuss them in your groups. Be sure to ask follow-up questions.

    1 Should you know where your food comes from and how it is produced?

    2 How much more would you be willing to spend on meat to ensure animals weren't abused?

    3 Do humans have the right to use animals as they want? Why or why not?

    4 Are all animals the same? How do you choose which should be treated better?

    5 Is the pain or suffering of an animal the same as that of a human? How do you decide?

    6 Would you eat meat even if you had to kill the animal yourself?

    7 Are there any animals you wouldn't eat or wear or ride? Which? Why not?

    8 Are there any uses of animals you would ban if you could? Which? Why?

I don't really worry about …

I'd be happy to spend …

I don't think I could kill a … but I might be able to kill a …

I wouldn't eat … because …

I would never …

I think it's important to think about …

2 Report the results of your discussion to the class. Answer follow-up questions from your classmates.

I see what you're saying. But have you thought about …?

Can you explain your reasons for …?

Quotable quotes
Final thoughts . . .

I think it would be lovely if we stopped this whole notion of pets altogether.

Ingrid Newkirk
Animal rights activist

1 If we followed this suggestion, what would happen to dogs and cats?

2 How is this quote connected to the topic of this unit?

3 Do you believe that animals would be better off if they had no contact with humans?

Activities

Unit 7, page 54, Researching a topic

A Information gathering

Student B: look at the table below. Ask your partner for the missing information and complete the table.

Los Angeles to New York		
Transportation	Carbon footprint (kg)	Unit
airplane		
small car	700	per vehicle
big SUV		
bus	100	per seat
train		
bicycle	40	per person

Unit 8, page 62, Researching a topic

A Information gathering

Answers

Movie	Type of disaster
Contagion	disease
Dante's Peak	volcano
Don't Look Up	comet
Noah	flood
San Andreas	earthquake
Terminator 3: Rise of the Machines	nuclear war
The Day After Tomorrow	climate change
The Perfect Storm	hurricane/typhoon
The Poseidon Adventure	tsunami
Titanic	vehicle accident
Twister	tornado
War of the Worlds	alien attack

Core vocabulary: keywords

Unit-by-unit list

Unit 1
acquire
equivalent
estimate
exposure
multiple
per
regional
researcher
retain
struggle

Unit 2
absolutely
administration
cite
collapse
dominate
elementary
outcome
primary
severe
vital

Unit 3
era
estate
forecast
household
increasingly
largely
previous
rural
ultimately
wage

Unit 4
critic
decade
expansion
guarantee
launch
overall
reduction
secure
settlement
southern

Unit 5
ban/banned
boost
consequence
current
extremely
facility
historic
suspend
tournament
yield

Unit 6
analysis
annual
budget
compensation
controversial
debt
profit
recruit
revenue
sum

Unit 7
conclude
massive
pace
predict
significant
stem
substantial
tackle
thus
voter

Unit 8
acknowledge
advocate
alternative
dispute
extraordinary
flood
initial
prisoner
prospect
theory

Unit 9
approve
assess
asset
comparison
guard
investigation
obviously
priority
truly
virtually

Unit 10
context
elsewhere
equipment
pose
procedure
prompt
represent
restore
surgery
urge

Unit 11
appropriate
capture
crops
declare
decline
eliminate
pursue
religious
requirement
threaten

Unit 12
abuse
alongside
circumstance
complaint
investment
purchase
shareholder
sort
strategy
vehicle

Alphabetical list

A
absolutely
abuse
acknowledge
acquire
administration
advocate
alongside
alternative
analysis
annual
appropriate
approve
assess
asset

B
ban/banned
boost
budget

C
capture
circumstance
cite
collapse
comparison
compensation
complaint
conclude
consequence
context
controversial
critic
crops
current

D
debt
decade
declare
decline
dispute
dominate

E
elementary
eliminate
elsewhere
equipment
equivalent
era
estate
estimate
expansion
exposure
extraordinary
extremely

F
facility
flood
forecast

G
guarantee
guard

H
historic
household

I
increasingly
initial
investigation
investment

L
largely
launch

M
massive
multiple

O
obviously
outcome
overall

P
pace
per
pose
predict
previous
primary
priority
prisoner
procedure
profit
prompt
prospect
purchase
pursue

R
recruit
reduction
regional
religious
represent
requirement
researcher
restore
retain
revenue
rural

S
secure
settlement

severe
shareholder
significant
sort
southern
stem
strategy
struggle
substantial
sum
surgery
suspend

T
tackle
theory
threaten
thus
tournament
truly

U
ultimately
urge

V
vehicle
virtually
vital
voter

W
wage

Y
yield

Credits

In Focus 2

2024年1月20日　初版第1刷発行
2024年8月30日　初版第3刷発行

著　者　Charles Browne
Brent Culligan
Joseph Phillips

発行者　福　岡　正　人

発行所　株式会社　金星堂

（〒101-0051）　東京都千代田区神田神保町 3-21
Tel　(03) 3263-3828 （営業部）
(03) 3263-3997 （編集部）
Fax　(03) 3263-0716
https://www.kinsei-do.co.jp

編集担当　Richard Walker・Takahiro Imakado　　Printed in Japan
印刷所・製本所／シナノ書籍印刷株式会社

ISBN978-4-7647-4194-2　　C1082